SALVATION

AND THE LAW

What the Law Can Do—and What
Salvation Alone Can Accomplish

Dr. Ed Grefiel

**"The Law reveals the truth.
Christ fulfills the Law.
Salvation restores life"**

DEDICATION

This book is dedicated to all who have lived under fear, striving to be right with God yet never finding rest.

To those who have tried to obey without life,

who have trusted rules more than relationship,
who have felt condemned even while seeking God sincerely—
this is for you.

It is also dedicated to those who hunger for truth,

who refuse shallow answers,
and who are willing to follow Scripture wherever it leads—
even when it leads away from systems and toward a Person.

Above all, this book is dedicated to Jesus Christ,

the fulfillment of the Law,
the satisfaction of justice,
the healer of sin,
and the giver of life.

May every reader move

from fear to faith,

from striving to rest,

from law to life,

and from distance to reconciliation in Him.

FOREWORD

Every human being should know that there is a big gap between them and the Holy God. Each one must acknowledge that they need a Mediator to connect them to the Most Holy God. Disregarding this need leads them to eternal damnation when they die and are not reconciled to their Creator.

People are confused about the Old Testament Law and their salvation. And many are still under the bondage of the Law of Moses, which our Lord Jesus Christ *"...wiped out the handwriting of requirements that was against us, which was contrary to us. And He has taken it out of the way, having nailed it to the cross"* (**Colossians 2:14**).

The work of the humble servant of God, Dr. Ed Grefiel, enlightens readers by how they will be grounded to the **knowledge of truth**. He differentiates between the Law of God given to Moses and how humanity comes to know that they are saved.

The finished work of Jesus Christ on the Cross of Calvary is our hope throughout eternity. **Make Him come and dwell in your heart** for He is our only access to **enter in Heaven**.

Dominador Viernes

Ptr. Life Christian Fellowship.

PREFACE

Why Law And Salvation Are Universal Questions

This book is the **third** in a twelve-part series on salvation titled:

"Steps of Faith: A Journey to Salvation for All"

This series is devoted to presenting salvation as Scripture reveals it—clearly, completely, and centered in Christ. Each book builds upon the previous, forming a unified progression that leads the reader from foundational truth to deeper understanding, and ultimately to life in Christ.

In the earlier part of this journey, we established that salvation is not a secondary doctrine but the **foundation** through which all truth must be understood. Scripture does not present salvation as one topic among many—it presents it as the center of God's redemptive work, the answer to humanity's condition, and the key to understanding life, truth, and purpose.

This book now turns to a question that stands at the center of human experience and biblical revelation:

What is the role of the Law in relation to salvation?

Why This Question Belongs to Everyone

Every person, regardless of background, lives with an awareness that life is not as it should be.

We recognize right and wrong.

We feel guilt—even when no one else sees.

We long for justice—even when we cannot fully define it.

We sense that something is broken—within us and around us.

These realities are not accidental. They point to a deeper truth:

Humanity lives under moral accountability before God.

Scripture reveals that this awareness exists even before written commandments:

"They show that the work of the law is written on their hearts, while their conscience also bears witness…"

— Romans 2:15

Yet this awareness is not a perfect guide. Conscience can be shaped, influenced, dulled, or even distorted:

"Their consciences are seared…"

— 1 Timothy 4:2

So while humanity senses truth, it does not fully possess it.

We are aware—but not complete.

We recognize—but cannot restore ourselves.

Why the Law Was Given

The Law was not the beginning of sin, nor the origin of accountability. Sin existed before the Law. Death reigned before commandments were written.

The Law was given to **make truth clear**:

"Through the law comes knowledge of sin."

— Romans 3:20

It defines transgression.

It exposes the heart.

It establishes justice.

But the Law also reveals its limitation:

"If a law had been given that could give life, then righteousness would indeed be by the law."

— Galatians 3:21

The Law can reveal—but it cannot restore.

It can define guilt—but it cannot remove it.

It can demand justice—but it cannot give life.

Why Salvation Is Necessary

If the Law reveals the truth but cannot heal the condition, then the question becomes unavoidable:

What can restore what has been broken?

Scripture answers clearly:

"For Christ is the end of the law for righteousness to everyone who believes."

— Romans 10:4

Salvation is not an improvement of human effort.

It is not a continuation of the Law.

It is the **fulfillment of what the Law required** and the **restoration of life through Christ**.

The Purpose of This Book

This book follows Scripture's own progression:

Sin → Law → Transgression → Christ → Life

It seeks to answer:

- What the Law can do

- What the Law cannot do

- Why sin exists beyond written commandments

- How transgression brings charge and judgment

- Why Christ fulfills the Law completely

- And how salvation alone restores life

This is written not only for the church, but for **all people**—because the questions of guilt, justice, truth, and life belong to every human being.

A Final Word Before You Begin

You may come to this book with different assumptions:

- That obedience is the way to life

- That law and salvation are the same

- That guilt must be managed or hidden

- Or that there is no clear answer at all

Scripture does not leave these questions unanswered.

But it does not lead us to a system—

it leads us to a **Person**.

"You will know the truth, and the truth will set you free."

— John 8:32

As you read, the invitation is not merely to understand the Law, but to encounter **the life that the Law could never give— the life that is found in Christ alone.**

CONTENTS

PART I — BEFORE THE LAW: GOD, TRUTH, AND THE HUMAN CONDITION

PART II — THE LAW GIVEN: GOD'S REVELATION AND ITS PURPOSE

INTRODUCTION

The Question Scripture Answers For Every Person

Why humans feel accountable before God even before knowing His Law

Long before a person encounters Scripture, hears a sermon, or learns the language of faith, a quiet awareness is already at work within the human experience. People everywhere sense accountability—an inward recognition that some things are right and others are wrong, that actions carry moral weight, and that life somehow stands under evaluation. This awareness is not limited to religious communities. It appears across cultures, generations, and worldviews.

Why is this so?

Why do people feel guilt even when no one is watching? Why does wrongdoing feel heavier than mere mistake? Why does justice seem necessary, yet never fully satisfied by human systems? And why do efforts to silence moral awareness or redefine right and wrong never fully succeed?

Scripture does not introduce these questions; it explains them.

The Bible teaches that accountability does not begin with written law. It begins with God. Humanity was created to live in relationship with Him—aligned with His truth, goodness, and life. Because of this, moral awareness exists even where explicit commandments have not yet been revealed. Scripture affirms that human beings live as moral creatures before they live as law-informed ones:

"When Gentiles, who do not have the law, by nature do what the law requires… they show that the work of the law is written on their hearts, while their conscience also bears witness."

— Romans 2:14–15

At the same time, Scripture is careful in how it speaks about conscience. Conscience is real, but it is not an infallible guide. It bears witness to moral awareness, yet it is shaped by upbringing, culture, environment, repeated behavior, and the presence or absence of revelation. Because of this, conscience can accuse wrongly, excuse wrongly, or become dulled. Scripture acknowledges these realities explicitly:

- A weak conscience (1 Corinthians 8:7)

- A defiled conscience (Titus 1:15)

- A seared conscience (1 Timothy 4:2)

Conscience explains why humans feel accountable; it does not define what they are accountable to. Scripture alone provides that standard.

This is why the Bible never grounds moral authority in conscience itself, but in God's revelation. Conscience testifies that humanity lives under accountability; God's Word reveals the source, meaning, and measure of that accountability.

When the Law appears in Scripture, it does not introduce morality into a morally neutral world. Rather, it reveals, clarifies, and names what already exists. The Law defines transgression, exposes sin, and brings accountability into sharp focus. Yet Scripture is equally clear that the Law was never given to save:

"Through the law comes knowledge of sin."

— Romans 3:20

The Law tells the truth about the human condition, but it cannot heal what it exposes. Scripture itself declares this limitation:

"If a law had been given that could give life, then righteousness would indeed be by the law."

— Galatians 3:21

This is where salvation enters the story—not as a religious add-on, but as God's necessary response to a condition the Law can only reveal. Salvation addresses both realities humanity experiences: the guilt the Law defines and the brokenness that moral awareness senses. In Jesus Christ, justice is fulfilled without being denied, condemnation is ended without ignoring truth, and life is restored where death once reigned:

"There is therefore now no condemnation for those who are in Christ Jesus."

— Romans 8:1

This book is written for every person who has felt the weight of accountability, the restlessness of unresolved guilt, or the longing for justice and peace that rules alone cannot provide. It is written to show why Scripture speaks so directly to the human condition, and why salvation is not an escape from accountability, but its fulfillment.

The question Scripture answers is not merely religious.

It is profoundly human.

Why do we feel accountable?

Because we were created by God and for truth.

Why does the Law matter?

Because it reveals what is broken.

Why does salvation matter?

Because only God can restore what the Law exposes.

This is the journey we will take together.

PART I

Before The Law: God, Truth, And The Human Condition

Introduction to Part I

Before Scripture ever records a command, a statute, or a covenantal law, it first reveals God—who He is, what He is like, and how humanity exists in relation to Him. This order is intentional and foundational. Law does not create truth, goodness, or justice; it flows from them. And truth, goodness, and justice flow from God Himself.

Part I establishes a critical biblical reality: the human problem did not begin with the Law, and God's truth did not begin with commands. Sin, accountability, moral awareness, and death existed before Sinai—not because humanity had a written code, but because humanity was created in relationship with a holy God.

This section answers essential questions that shape everything that follows:

- *Why does moral accountability exist before written law?*

- *Why does Scripture speak of sin before commandments?*

- *Why did God give the Law if sin already existed?*

- *Why does conscience accuse, yet remain unreliable?*

- *Why must salvation address more than rule-breaking?*

By grounding these questions in Scripture, Part I prepares the reader to understand what the Law can do—

and why it was never meant to save.

Chapter 1 — God Before Law

The Bible does not begin with rules. It begins with God.

"In the beginning, God created the heavens and the earth."
— Genesis 1:1

This opening declaration establishes the most important truth of all: God precedes everything—including law. Truth, goodness, justice, and righteousness are not abstract ideals or social constructs; they are rooted in the nature of God Himself.

Because God is:

- Truth (He does not lie),

- Good (He is not morally neutral),

- Just (He does not overlook evil),

law is not an invention to control humanity but an expression of who God is. Law flows from God's nature; it does not define it.

This chapter establishes Scripture—not human reasoning, culture, or philosophy—as the starting point for understanding morality, accountability, and justice. Without God as the foundation, law becomes arbitrary, shifting, or oppressive. With God as the foundation, law reflects moral reality.

Chapter 2 — What Scripture Means by Sin

Before Scripture speaks of law-breaking, it speaks of sin.

Sin, biblically understood, is not merely doing something forbidden. It is nonconformity to God Himself—a deviation from His truth, will, character, and design. This is why Scripture can speak of sin long before any written law exists.

"All have sinned and fall short of the glory of God."
— Romans 3:23

Sin is relational and ontological. It affects being, not merely behavior. Humanity's problem is not first legal guilt, but misalignment with God—a rupture in relationship that distorts desire, thought, and action.

This chapter clarifies why sin exists before written law and why law cannot be the ultimate solution. If sin were merely rule-breaking, law could fix it. But because sin is deeper than law, salvation must also be deeper.

Chapter 3 — Sin Before Moses

One of Scripture's most striking claims is that death reigned before the Law.

"Death reigned from Adam to Moses."

— Romans 5:14

This statement demands explanation. How could humanity be accountable without Torah? How could judgment occur without commandments?

Scripture answers by pointing to history itself: Adam's disobedience, Cain's violence, the corruption before the Flood, and the pride of Babel. These events occur before Sinai, yet God clearly responds to sin with judgment, mercy, and restraint.

This chapter demonstrates that accountability existed before codified law because humanity was already accountable to God. The Law did not introduce sin; it clarified and formalized it. Death, judgment, and moral responsibility existed because God's moral order already governed human life.

Chapter 4 — The Law Written on the Heart

If law was not written, why did humanity still experience guilt, accountability, and moral tension?

Scripture teaches that God placed a moral awareness within humanity—but never treats it as an infallible guide.

"They show that the work of the law is written on their hearts, while their conscience also bears witness."
— Romans 2:15

Conscience bears witness to accountability, but it does not define moral truth. It is shaped by culture, environment, repeated behavior, and revelation. Scripture speaks of weak, defiled, and seared consciences, showing that conscience can accuse wrongly or fail to accuse at all.

This chapter carefully distinguishes:

- Moral awareness from moral authority

- Conscience from God's revealed truth

- Inner witness from objective righteousness

God testifies not only through conscience, but through creation, history, and ultimately His Word. Conscience explains why humans feel accountable; Scripture explains what they are accountable to.

Why Part I Matters

Part I establishes a non-negotiable biblical truth:
The Law did not create morality, sin, or accountability.

God did.

Only after this foundation is clear can we rightly understand:

- Why the Law was given,

- What the Law can do,

- Why salvation must do what the Law cannot.

CHAPTER 1

God Before Law

Before Scripture ever speaks of commandments, statutes, or covenants, it speaks of God. This order is deliberate and foundational. Law does not stand at the beginning of reality; God does. To reverse this order—to begin with law rather than with God—is to misunderstand both law and salvation.

"In the beginning, God created the heavens and the earth."

— Genesis 1:1

Scripture opens not with rules, but with revelation. God is not introduced as a lawgiver first, but as Creator, Source, and Lord. Everything that follows—including moral order, accountability, and law—flows from who God is.

God as the Source of Truth, Goodness, and Justice

Truth, goodness, and justice are not abstract ideals floating above God, nor are they products of human consensus. They are rooted in God's very nature. Scripture consistently presents God as the standard by which all things are measured.

- God is true and cannot lie (Numbers 23:19)

- God is good, and all goodness flows from Him (Psalm 119:68)

- God is just, and all His ways are right (Deuteronomy 32:4)

This means morality is not arbitrary. Right and wrong are not determined by culture, majority opinion, or historical moment. They are grounded in the unchanging character of God. When Scripture speaks of righteousness, it is not referring merely to correct behavior, but to conformity with God Himself.

This is a crucial foundation:

God does not conform to law; law conforms to God.

Reflection:

If goodness and justice are rooted in God's nature, how does that challenge the idea that morality can be defined independently of God?

Why Law Flows from God's Nature

Because God is holy, truthful, and just, His will carries moral weight. Law, therefore, is not an external system imposed upon God's character; it is an expression of that character in a form humanity can understand.

Scripture affirms this explicitly:

"The law is holy, and the commandment is holy and righteous and good." — **Romans 7:12**

The Law is good because God is good. The Law is just because God is just. The Law is truthful because God is truthful. Law is not opposed to grace by nature; it is opposed only to the misuse that treats it as a means of life rather than a witness to truth.

This distinction matters deeply. When law is detached from God's nature, it becomes:

- Arbitrary

- Oppressive

- Fear-producing

- Lifeless

But when law is understood as flowing from God, its proper role becomes clear: it reveals, defines, and bears witness—it does not save.

Reflection:

How does viewing the Law as an expression of God's nature (rather than a tool for earning righteousness) reshape your understanding of obedience?

Scripture as the Starting Point—Not Human Systems

Because law flows from God, Scripture—not human systems—must be the starting point for understanding morality, sin, and justice. Philosophy, culture, and conscience can describe human moral experience, but they cannot define moral truth.

Scripture repeatedly warns against replacing God's revelation with human wisdom:

"There is a way that seems right to a man, but its end is the way to death."
— Proverbs 14:12

Human systems of law and ethics can restrain evil and organize society, but they cannot heal the human heart or restore alignment with God. This is because the deepest problem humanity faces is not lack of regulation, but alienation from the Source of life.

By beginning with God, Scripture establishes a non-negotiable truth: accountability exists because God exists. Law is meaningful only because it reflects a moral reality that precedes it. Without God, law loses its grounding; with God, law finds its proper place.

Reflection:

Where are you most tempted to let culture, experience, or personal reasoning take precedence over Scripture in defining right and wrong?

Why This Order Matters for Salvation

Starting with God before law protects the gospel from distortion. If law comes first, salvation becomes escape from punishment or achievement through compliance. But if God comes first, salvation is understood as restoration of relationship, healing of misalignment, and life returned to its source.

This is why Scripture never presents salvation as law-management. It presents salvation as reconciliation to God through Jesus Christ.

"This is eternal life, that they know you, the only true God, and Jesus Christ whom you have sent."
— John 17:3

Eternal life is relational before it is legal. And because God precedes law, salvation must also precede and transcend it.

Chapter Summary

- God is the source of truth, goodness, and justice

- Law flows from God's nature; it does not define Him

- Scripture, not human systems, is the foundation of moral truth

- Beginning with God preserves the true meaning of law and salvation

Final Reflection:

If God—not law—is the foundation of morality and life, how should that shape the way you understand sin, obedience, and salvation as you continue reading?

End of Chapter 1

CHAPTER 2

What Scripture Means By Sin

Before Scripture ever speaks of commands broken, it speaks of relationship broken. Sin, in the Bible, is not first a legal category; it is a relational and ontological reality. To misunderstand this is to misunderstand why law was given—and why salvation must do more than regulate behavior.

"All have sinned and fall short of the glory of God."
— Romans 3:23

This verse does not define sin as rule-breaking. It defines sin as falling short of God's glory—of who God is. Scripture consistently presents sin as a failure to conform to God Himself.

Sin as Nonconformity to God

At its most basic level, sin is nonconformity to God—to His truth, character, will, and ways. God is not measured by law; law reflects Him. Therefore, sin is not merely disobedience to commands but departure from God's nature.

Scripture makes this clear:

"Be holy, for I am holy."

— Leviticus 11:44

Holiness is grounded in who God is, not merely in what He commands. To sin is to live out of alignment with that holiness—to think, desire, choose, or act in ways that do not reflect God.

This is why sin can exist even when no explicit command has been violated. A heart that distrusts God, resists truth, or seeks autonomy is already misaligned, even before any boundary is crossed.

Reflection:

If sin is defined by nonconformity to God rather than mere rule-breaking, how does that change the way you understand repentance?

Sin as Relational and Ontological Misalignment

Scripture consistently portrays sin as something that affects being, not only behavior. Sin is not simply something we do; it is a condition that distorts how we relate to God, to others, and to ourselves.

This relational rupture appears early in Scripture:

"Your iniquities have made a separation between you and your God."

— Isaiah 59:2

Sin separates because it disrupts alignment with the Source of life. When relationship with God is broken, consequences follow naturally—alienation, corruption, and ultimately death.

Paul describes this condition clearly:

"You were dead in the trespasses and sins in which you once walked."

— Ephesians 2:1

Death here is not first physical; it is relational and spiritual. Sin disconnects humanity from God's life. This is why Scripture treats salvation not merely as forgiveness of acts, but as new creation, reconciliation, and restoration.

Reflection:

In what ways does Scripture's description of sin as a condition challenge the idea that moral improvement alone can solve the human problem?

Why Sin Exists Before Written Law

One of the clearest biblical proofs that sin is deeper than law is this: sin existed before the Law was given.

Scripture states this explicitly:

"Sin indeed was in the world before the law was given."

— **Romans 5:13**

If sin were merely the violation of written commandments, this statement would make no sense. Yet Scripture repeatedly speaks of sin, judgment, and death long before Sinai.

From the beginning:

- Adam's disobedience introduced sin and death (Genesis 3)

- Cain's violence was judged as sin (Genesis 4:7–11)

- The Flood came because human wickedness was great (Genesis 6:5)

None of these events occurred under the Mosaic Law. Accountability existed because humanity was accountable to God, not because a legal code had been issued.

Paul draws the conclusion plainly:

"Death reigned from Adam to Moses."

— Romans 5:14

Death reigns because sin reigns—and sin reigns because humanity is misaligned with God. Law did not introduce sin; it clarified it. Law did not cause death; it exposed the reality already at work.

Reflection:

Why is it important for understanding salvation that sin existed—and was judged—before the Law?

Why This Matters for Salvation

If sin were merely legal guilt, law could resolve it. But because sin is relational and ontological, law alone can never heal it. This is why Scripture never presents salvation as rule-keeping, but as reconciliation to God.

"While we were enemies we were reconciled to God by the death of his Son."

— Romans 5:10

Salvation addresses the deeper problem: misalignment with God. Forgiveness answers guilt; new life restores relationship. The Law can reveal sin, but only Christ can remove it and restore alignment.

Chapter Summary

- Sin is nonconformity to God, not merely disobedience to rules

- Sin is relational and ontological, affecting being and relationship

- Sin existed before written law because accountability existed before law

- Law reveals sin; salvation heals the condition sin creates

Final Reflection:

If sin is fundamentally misalignment with God, what must salvation accomplish that law never could?

End of Chapter 2

CHAPTER 3

Sin Before Moses

One of the clearest demonstrations that sin is deeper than written law is Scripture's own testimony that sin and judgment existed long before the Law was given at Sinai. If sin were merely the violation of codified commandments, there could be no guilt, no judgment, and no death prior to Moses. Yet the biblical record tells a different story.

"Death reigned from Adam to Moses."
— Romans 5:14

This single statement forces a crucial conclusion: accountability precedes Torah. Humanity stood responsible before God not because a law code had been issued, but because humanity lived in relationship to God.

Adam: Sin Without a Legal Code

The first sin recorded in Scripture occurs before any covenantal law existed.

"The LORD God commanded the man..."
— Genesis 2:16–17

Adam's sin was not the violation of a complex legal system. It was a relational breach—a turning away from God's word in distrust and autonomy. The consequence was immediate and severe:

- Shame entered

- Fellowship was broken

- Death became humanity's destiny

"In the day that you eat of it you shall surely die."
— Genesis 2:17

This death was not first physical; it was relational and spiritual, later culminating in physical death. Adam's case shows that sin is fundamentally misalignment with God, not merely law-breaking.

Reflection:

If Adam was accountable without Torah, what does that reveal about the true source of moral responsibility?

Cain: Sin Identified and Judged Without Law

Cain's murder of Abel occurs generations before Moses. Yet God clearly identifies Cain's action as sin and holds him accountable.

"Sin is crouching at the door. Its desire is contrary to you, but you must rule over it."

— Genesis 4:7

Notice what God does not say:

- He does not cite a statute

- He does not quote a commandment

- He does not reference a law code

Instead, God addresses Cain's moral responsibility directly. Cain knows what he is doing, and God judges accordingly.

"The voice of your brother's blood is crying to me from the ground."

— Genesis 4:10

Here we see that accountability is rooted in God's justice, not in written law.

Reflection:

Why does Scripture hold Cain fully accountable even without explicit commandments?

The Flood: Universal Judgment Before Sinai

By the time of the Flood, Scripture describes humanity's condition in unmistakable terms:

"The LORD saw that the wickedness of man was great in the earth, and that every intention of the thoughts of his heart was only evil continually." — **Genesis 6:5**

God's judgment through the Flood was not arbitrary. It was a response to pervasive sin, corruption, and violence—again, without reference to Mosaic Law.

This confirms a vital truth: God judges sin as sin, not merely as transgression of written statutes. Humanity's accountability was universal because God's moral order was universal.

Reflection:

What does the Flood reveal about the seriousness of sin apart from legal definitions?

Babel: Pride, Autonomy, and Divine Response

The Tower of Babel reveals another dimension of sin before law: collective pride and autonomous ambition.

"Come, let us make a name for ourselves."
— Genesis 11:4

Here, sin is not an isolated act but a shared posture of self-exaltation. God responds by confusing languages and scattering nations—not because a law was broken, but because humanity was united in rebellion against divine authority.

Babel shows that sin includes:

- Pride

- Self-sufficiency

- Rejection of God's ordering

None of these require Torah to be sinful.

Reflection:

How does Babel challenge the idea that sin is only personal or individual?

Why Death Reigned Without Torah

Paul's explanation is decisive:

"Sin indeed was in the world before the law was given."
— Romans 5:13

Death reigns where sin reigns—not where law exists. The Law later clarifies sin and defines transgression, but it does not create the problem it reveals.

Death reigns because:

- Humanity is misaligned with God

- Relationship with the Source of life is broken

- Corruption spreads apart from restoration

Law can expose this reality; it cannot reverse it.

Scriptural Evidence of Accountability Before Sinai

Scripture consistently presents God as judging, restraining, and engaging humanity long before Moses:

- God warns, judges, and shows mercy

- God establishes covenants (Noah, Abraham)

- God holds individuals and nations accountable

All of this occurs before the Law.

This establishes a foundational truth for the entire book:

Accountability is grounded in God's nature and humanity's relationship to Him—not in the presence of a written code.

Why This Matters for Understanding the Law

If sin, accountability, and death existed before the Law, then the Law must serve a different purpose than creating morality or introducing guilt. It was given to:

- Reveal sin clearly

- Define transgression formally

- Prepare the way for salvation

Understanding this prevents both legalism and lawlessness.

Chapter Summary

- Sin existed before Moses and before written law

- Adam, Cain, the Flood, and Babel demonstrate accountability without Torah

- Death reigned because sin reigned, not because law existed

- Law clarifies sin; it does not create it

Final Reflection:

If God held humanity accountable before the Law, how should that shape our understanding of why the Law was later given—and why salvation must go beyond it?

End of Chapter 3

CHAPTER 4

The Law Written On The Heart

Before the Law was given at Sinai, Scripture already speaks of moral awareness, accountability, and judgment among peoples who had never received the Torah. This reality does not mean that humanity possessed an internal law equal to God's revealed Word. Rather, it means that God testified to Himself through creation and through a moral awareness within the human person—an awareness Scripture carefully describes, limits, and submits to divine revelation.

This chapter clarifies three truths Scripture holds together without contradiction:

- Humans possess moral awareness.

- That awareness (conscience) is real but not infallible.

- God's revealed truth—not conscience—defines righteousness, sin, and justice.

Conscience in Scripture

Scripture acknowledges conscience as an inner faculty that bears witness to moral awareness. The New Testament term commonly translated "conscience" refers to an inner knowing that evaluates one's actions and motives. Yet Scripture never treats conscience as an independent moral authority or final judge.

"They show that the work of the law is written on their hearts, while their conscience also bears witness, and their conflicting thoughts accuse or even excuse them."

— Romans 2:15

Notice the language: conscience bears witness. It testifies; it does not legislate. It responds; it does not define. Scripture consistently places conscience under God's truth, not above it.

This is why the Bible speaks of conscience in varying conditions:

- A weak conscience (1 Corinthians 8:7)

- A defiled conscience (Titus 1:15)

- A seared conscience (1 Timothy 4:2)

If conscience were a reliable moral authority, such descriptions would make no sense. Scripture teaches instead that conscience is formable—shaped by culture, environment, repeated behavior, and the presence or absence of revelation. It can accuse wrongly, excuse wrongly, or fall silent altogether.

For this reason, conscience explains why humans feel accountable, but it does not explain what they are accountable to. That standard comes only from God's revealed truth.

Reflection:

In what ways have culture or habit shaped your moral instincts—and how does Scripture correct or refine them?

Moral Awareness Among the Nations

Scripture affirms that peoples outside Israel possessed genuine moral awareness and were held accountable by God—even without the Mosaic Law. This accountability was not based on possessing Torah, but on responding to the truth God made known.

"For although they knew God, they did not honor him as God or give thanks to him…" — **Romans 1:21**

Paul's argument is not that the nations lacked knowledge entirely, but that they suppressed what was known. This knowledge included:

- Awareness of God's power and divinity

- Recognition of right and wrong

- Responsibility to honor God

This explains why Scripture can speak of judgment among the nations without appealing to Mosaic statutes. Moral awareness existed; accountability followed. Yet Scripture never equates

23

this awareness with possessing God's Law. Awareness increases responsibility, but it does not replace revelation.

Reflection:

Why does Scripture hold people accountable for suppressing truth rather than for lacking information?

God's Testimony in Creation and the Human Heart

Scripture teaches that God testifies to Himself through creation and through the human person. This testimony establishes accountability, not salvation.

"What can be known about God is plain to them, because God has shown it to them."
— Romans 1:19

Creation reveals God's power and order; the human heart responds with awareness and responsibility. Yet neither creation nor conscience can define the fullness of God's righteousness or provide the means of restoration.

This is why Scripture insists on revelation. General testimony explains why humanity is accountable; special revelation explains how humanity is redeemed.

"The heavens declare the glory of God."

— Psalm 19:1

Creation declares glory; Scripture declares the way of life.

Reflection:

How does recognizing the limits of creation and conscience protect the gospel from becoming moralism?

What "The Law Written on the Heart" Does—and Does Not Mean

When Scripture speaks of "the work of the law written on the heart," it does not mean:

- That humans possess an internal copy of God's Law

- That conscience defines righteousness

- That salvation can be achieved apart from revelation

It does mean:

- Humans are moral beings created accountable to God

- God's moral order is not arbitrary

- Humanity is responsible even before written law

Conscience witnesses to accountability; Scripture defines truth; Christ restores life.

Why This Matters for Understanding the Law

This chapter guards against two equal errors:

- Moral relativism, which elevates conscience above truth

- Legalism, which assumes morality begins only with written law

Scripture rejects both. God's moral reality precedes the Law, but the Law clarifies and defines that reality. Conscience may awaken awareness, but only God's Word reveals righteousness—and only Christ heals the heart.

Chapter Summary

- Conscience is real, but not infallible

- Moral awareness exists among all peoples

- God testifies through creation and the human heart

- Conscience witnesses to accountability; Scripture defines truth

- The Law clarifies sin; salvation restores alignment

Final Reflection:

If conscience can witness to accountability but cannot define truth, where must we turn to rightly understand sin, righteousness, and life?

End of Chapter 4

PART II

The Law Given: God's Revelation And Its Purpose

Introduction to Part II

If sin, accountability, and death existed before the Law, then a crucial question follows: Why did God give the Law at all?

Part II answers this question directly from Scripture—without reducing the Law to legalism or dismissing it as obsolete.

The Law was not God's attempt to save humanity by regulation. Nor was it an experiment that failed. Scripture presents the Law as holy, purposeful, and limited—a divine revelation given at a particular moment in redemptive history to accomplish what only law can do, while preparing the way for what only salvation can accomplish.

This section shows:

- Why the Law was added, not foundational

- What the Law reveals that humanity could not see clearly

- How the Law turns sin into transgression

- Why condemnation arises under law

- Why the Law must give way to fulfillment in Christ

Part II establishes the Law's true role, so it is neither misused as a savior nor rejected as unnecessary.

Chapter 5 — Why God Gave the Law

Scripture does not leave the purpose of the Law ambiguous. Paul states it plainly:

"Why then the law? It was added because of transgressions."

— Galatians 3:19

The Law was added—which means it was not original to creation and not essential for moral existence. Its purpose was covenantal and revelatory, not salvific. God gave the Law to Israel to define boundaries, clarify guilt, and expose humanity's need—not to produce righteousness or life.

This chapter explores how the Law functioned within God's covenant with Israel and why Scripture insists that the Law was never a mechanism of salvation.

Reflection:

If God never intended the Law to save, why is it so often treated as if it were?

Chapter 6 — What the Law Reveals

The Law is a revealer. It does not create sin; it makes sin known.

"Through the law comes knowledge of sin."
— Romans 3:20

The Law exposes the heart by bringing God's moral will into sharp focus. What conscience sensed vaguely, the Law names clearly. It shows not only what is wrong, but who we are in relation to God.

Yet exposure is not healing. The Law clarifies guilt, but it does not cure corruption. This chapter explains why the Law can diagnose the problem perfectly while remaining powerless to fix it.

Reflection:

Why is exposure necessary—even when it cannot provide the solution?

Chapter 7 — From Sin to Transgression

One of the Law's most significant effects is that it transforms sin into transgression.

"Where there is no law there is no transgression."

— Romans 4:15

Sin is misalignment with God; transgression is the violation of a known command. By revealing God's will explicitly, the Law turns moral failure into chargeable offense. Accountability increases with revelation.

This chapter clarifies the biblical distinction between sin and transgression and explains why increased knowledge brings increased responsibility—without making the Law the source of sin.

Reflection:

How does knowing God's will more clearly increase responsibility without creating guilt?

Chapter 8 — The Charge and Condemnation of Transgression

When transgression occurs, the Law does not merely observe—it judges.

"Cursed be everyone who does not abide by all things written in the Book of the Law, and do them."

— Galatians 3:10

The Law functions as witness and judge, pronouncing guilt and condemnation where commands are violated. This condemnation is not cruelty; it is the lawful outcome of justice. Scripture insists that justice must be satisfied, not ignored.

This chapter explains why condemnation arises under the Law and why forgiveness without justice would contradict God's righteousness—setting the stage for Christ's redemptive work.

Reflection:

Why must justice be satisfied rather than dismissed for salvation to be meaningful?

Chapter 9 — The Limits of the Law

Scripture honors the Law's holiness while declaring its limits unmistakably.

"If a law had been given that could give life, then righteousness would indeed be by the law." — **Galatians 3:21**

Obedience can restrain behavior, but it cannot produce life. Law can regulate conduct, but it cannot transform the heart. The Law's inability to save is not a flaw—it is a boundary set by God Himself.

This chapter explains why restraint is not transformation, why effort cannot produce righteousness, and why the Law must yield to fulfillment in Christ.

Reflection:

How does recognizing the Law's limitation protect us from both legalism and despair?

Why Part II Matters

Part II establishes a decisive biblical truth:

The Law reveals the problem with precision—but it was never meant to be the cure.

Only after the Law's purpose and limits are understood can salvation be rightly proclaimed—not as lawlessness, but as fulfillment, justice satisfied, and life restored.

CHAPTER 5

Why God Gave The Law

If sin, accountability, and death existed before the Law, then the question is unavoidable: Why did God give the Law at all? Scripture answers this question directly—and decisively—so that the Law is neither exalted as a savior nor dismissed as unnecessary.

"Why then the law? It was added because of transgressions."
— **Galatians 3:19**

This single sentence establishes three critical truths:

- The Law was added (it was not foundational to creation).

- The Law addressed transgressions, not the origin of sin.

- The Law had a specific purpose within God's redemptive plan.

"The Law Was Added Because of Transgressions"

Paul's wording matters. The Law was not given to create morality, nor to produce righteousness. It was given to clarify, define, and formalize accountability.

Before the Law:

- Sin existed as misalignment with God.

- Death reigned because relationship with the Source of life was broken.

With the Law:

- Sin became transgression—the violation of a known, revealed command.

- Guilt became chargeable.

- Accountability became undeniable.

"Where there is no law there is no transgression."
— Romans 4:15

The Law does not introduce sin; it introduces clarity. What conscience sensed vaguely, the Law names precisely. What was once internal becomes accountable before God and community. In this way, the Law functions as revelation—not as remedy.

Reflection:

How does understanding the Law as "added" protect us from treating it as the foundation of salvation?

Covenant Purpose, Not a Salvation Mechanism

Scripture presents the Law as a covenantal gift to Israel, not a universal ladder to righteousness. God gave the Law to shape a people, preserve worship, restrain injustice, and prepare the way for the Messiah.

"The law is holy, and the commandment is holy and righteous and good."

— Romans 7:12

The Law is **good** because God is **good**. But Scripture is equally clear: good does not mean saving.

"By works of the law no human being will be justified in his sight."

— Romans 3:20

If the Law could save, Christ would not have been necessary. But the Law was never intended to grant life. Its role was to reveal God's righteousness and expose humanity's inability to meet that standard on its own.

This is why Scripture insists that righteousness comes apart from the Law, even while the Law bears witness to it:

"But now the righteousness of God has been manifested apart from the law… through faith in Jesus Christ."

— Romans 3:21–22

Reflection:

Why is it important to affirm the Law's goodness without assigning it a saving role?

What the Law Was Never Meant to Do

To understand the Law rightly, we must be just as clear about what it cannot do as about what it can do.

Scripture explicitly denies the Law's ability to:

- Give life

- Heal the heart

- Produce righteousness

- Restore relationship with God

"If a law had been given that could give life, then righteousness would indeed be by the law."

— Galatians 3:21

The Law can restrain behavior, but it cannot transform desire. It can expose sin, but it cannot remove it. It can pronounce judgment, but it cannot grant mercy. These limits are not failures; they are boundaries set by God.

Because the Law cannot save, it performs a different, necessary function:

"So then, the law was our guardian to bring us to Christ."
— Galatians 3:24

The Law escorts humanity to the conclusion it cannot escape: we need salvation that law cannot provide.

Reflection:

How does recognizing what the Law was never meant to do deepen gratitude for Christ's finished work?

Why This Matters for Salvation

Misunderstanding the Law produces two opposite errors:

- Legalism, which treats the Law as a path to life

- Lawlessness, which treats the Law as irrelevant

Scripture rejects both. The Law reveals truth; salvation accomplishes restoration. The Law clarifies guilt; salvation satisfies justice. The Law exposes the problem; Christ provides the cure.

Understanding why God gave the Law allows us to honor it properly—without trusting it for what only Christ can do.

Chapter Summary

- The Law was added because of transgressions

- Its purpose was covenantal and revelatory, not salvific

- The Law clarifies guilt but cannot give life

- Its limits prepare the way for salvation in Christ

Final Reflection:

If the Law was given to reveal need rather than provide life, how should that shape the way you approach obedience, grace, and assurance as you continue reading?

End of Chapter 5

CHAPTER 6

What The Law Reveals

The Law's power lies not in what it gives, but in what it reveals. Scripture never presents the Law as a source of life; it presents it as a light—

bright enough to expose reality, but not designed to heal what it uncovers.

"Through the law comes knowledge of sin."
— Romans 3:20

This chapter clarifies the revelatory function of the Law: it makes sin known, exposes the heart, and clarifies guilt—

while remaining unable to restore what sin has damaged.

Knowledge of Sin

The Law names what conscience often senses but cannot define. Before the Law, humanity experienced moral awareness; with the Law, that awareness became explicit knowledge. God's commands turn vague intuition into clear recognition.

"I would not have known what it is to covet if the law had not said, 'You shall not covet.'"

— Romans 7:7

The Law does not create sinful desire; it reveals it. By articulating God's will, the Law draws a precise line between alignment and misalignment. What was once excusable ignorance becomes accountable knowledge. This is why the Law increases awareness without increasing righteousness.

Reflection:

Why is it necessary for sin to be clearly named before it can be rightly addressed?

Exposure of the Heart

The Law does more than evaluate actions; it reaches inward to expose desires, intentions, and motives. By forbidding not only outward acts but inward dispositions, the Law reveals the depth of the human problem.

"The law is spiritual, but I am of the flesh, sold under sin."

— Romans 7:14

When the Law commands love, fidelity, and truthfulness, it exposes how far the heart falls short. This exposure is not cruelty; it is truth-telling. The Law acts as a mirror—accurate and uncompromising—showing not only what we do, but who we are in need of renewal.

"The word of God... discerns the thoughts and intentions of the heart."

— Hebrews 4:12

Reflection:

How does the Law's exposure of inner motives challenge the idea that outward obedience alone is sufficient?

Why the Law Clarifies Guilt but Cannot Heal

Because the Law reveals God's righteous standard, it necessarily clarifies guilt when that standard is violated. This guilt is not subjective shame; it is objective accountability before God.

"All who rely on works of the law are under a curse."

— Galatians 3:10

Yet Scripture is equally clear about the Law's limitation:

"If a law had been given that could give life, then righteousness would indeed be by the law."

— Galatians 3:21

The Law can identify the disease but cannot provide the cure. It can restrain behavior, but it cannot transform desire. It can condemn wrongdoing, but it cannot restore relationship. Healing requires life, and life comes only from God.

This limitation is not a failure of the Law; it is its design. By clarifying guilt without offering healing, the Law drives humanity to seek salvation beyond itself.

"So then, the law was our guardian to bring us to Christ."

— Galatians 3:24

Reflection:

Why would God design the Law to expose guilt without providing healing?

Why This Matters for the Gospel

If the Law could heal, Christ would be unnecessary. But because the Law reveals without restoring, salvation must be something the Law cannot accomplish. The gospel does not deny the Law's verdict; it fulfills it. It does not ignore guilt; it answers it. And it does not leave the heart exposed; it renews it.

"For what the law could not do… God has done by sending his own Son."

— Romans 8:3

Understanding what the Law reveals protects us from two errors:

- Trusting the Law to heal what it can only expose

- Rejecting the Law because it exposes uncomfortable truth

Scripture calls us to embrace both revelation and redemption— each in its proper place.

Chapter Summary

- The Law brings clear knowledge of sin

- It exposes the heart, not just behavior

- It clarifies guilt before God

- It cannot heal or give life

- Its revelatory role prepares the way for salvation in Christ

Final Reflection:

If the Law reveals truth but cannot heal, where must healing come from—and how does that shape the way you respond to conviction?

End of Chapter 6

CHAPTER 7

From Sin To Transgression

Scripture makes a careful distinction between sin and transgression—a distinction essential for understanding why the Law was given and how accountability operates. Sin describes humanity's misalignment with God; transgression describes the violation of a known, revealed command. The Law does not create sin, but it converts sin into a chargeable offense by defining God's will with clarity.

"Where there is no law there is no transgression."

— Romans 4:15

This chapter explains that distinction, how revelation intensifies responsibility, and why increased light brings increased accountability.

The Biblical Distinction

Sin exists wherever human life departs from God's truth, character, and design. It is relational and ontological—affecting being and relationship before it affects conduct.

Transgression, by contrast, occurs when sin crosses a revealed boundary. It is sin named, defined, and legally charged because God has spoken.

Scripture holds both realities together:

"Sin indeed was in the world before the law was given."
— **Romans 5:13**

Sin existed before Sinai, but transgression requires law. This is why Adam could sin without Torah, and why Israel could transgress once Torah was given. The distinction protects us from two errors: denying sin where no law is present, and blaming the Law for creating sin.

Reflection:

Why is it important to distinguish between misalignment with God (sin) and violation of a known command (transgression)?

How Law Converts Sin into a Chargeable Offense

When God reveals His will explicitly, sin moves from the realm of misalignment into the realm of legal accountability. The Law names actions, sets boundaries, and attaches consequences. What conscience sensed, the Law defines; what was inward, the Law brings into the open.

Paul describes this effect personally:

"I would not have known what it is to covet if the law had not said, 'You shall not covet.'"
— **Romans 7:7**

The Law does not create desire; it exposes it. By revealing God's standard, the Law turns moral failure into a chargeable offense—not to condemn arbitrarily, but to clarify truth and justice.

This is why Scripture can say:

"The law brings wrath."
— **Romans 4:15**

Wrath arises not because the Law is evil, but because revealed righteousness confronts revealed disobedience.

Reflection:

How does the Law's clarity change the nature of responsibility compared to moral awareness alone?

Why Accountability Increases with Revelation

A consistent biblical principle is that responsibility increases with light. Revelation does not create guilt; it intensifies accountability by removing ignorance.

"That servant who knew his master's will but did not get ready… will receive a severe beating."

— Luke 12:47

This principle explains why Israel's accountability differed from that of the nations, and why believers are accountable to the fullness of the gospel. The more clearly God speaks, the more serious the response becomes.

Paul summarizes the dynamic:

"The law came in to increase the trespass."

— Romans 5:20

This does not mean God desired more sin. It means the Law made transgression unmistakable, so that salvation would be recognized as necessary and grace would be understood as truly gracious.

Reflection:

Why would God choose to increase accountability rather than reduce it?

Why This Distinction Matters

Failing to distinguish sin from transgression leads to confusion:

- Treating all guilt as legal, ignoring the deeper condition

- Treating grace as permission, ignoring accountability

- Misusing the Law either to condemn or to dismiss

Scripture avoids these errors by maintaining the distinction. Sin explains why humanity needs salvation; transgression explains why justice must be satisfied. The Law addresses transgression; Christ addresses both.

"Christ redeemed us from the curse of the law by becoming a curse for us."

— Galatians 3:13

Chapter Summary

- Sin is misalignment with God that exists before written law

- Transgression is sin that violates a revealed command

- The Law converts sin into a chargeable offense

- Accountability increases with revelation

- This distinction prepares the way for justice satisfied in Christ

Final Reflection:

If revelation increases accountability, how should grace shape our response to the truth we now know?

End of Chapter 7

CHAPTER 8

The Charge and Condemnation of Transgression

When sin becomes transgression, the Law does not remain silent. Scripture presents the Law as more than a moral guide—it functions as a witness and, in a real sense, a judge. Once God's will is clearly revealed, violation carries charge, guilt, and condemnation. This chapter explains why judgment under the Law is not cruelty, but justice—and why justice cannot simply be ignored.

"All who rely on works of the law are under a curse."
— Galatians 3:10

The Law as Witness and Judge

The Law testifies to what God has commanded and bears witness against those who violate it. Scripture consistently portrays the Law as standing in court, so to speak, establishing truth and rendering a verdict.

"Now we know that whatever the law says it speaks to those who are under the law, so that every mouth may be stopped, and the whole world may be held accountable to God." **— Romans 3:19**

The Law does not invent guilt; it confirms it. It does not accuse falsely; it exposes reality. When transgression occurs, the Law silences self-justification and establishes accountability before God.

This is why Scripture says the Law brings knowledge of sin, not life. It reveals the truth so clearly that denial becomes impossible.

Reflection:

Why is it necessary for accountability to be unmistakable rather than negotiable?

Curse, Guilt, and Judgment

Because the Law reflects God's holiness, violation carries real consequences. Scripture describes these consequences using strong language: curse, guilt, and judgment.

"Cursed be anyone who does not confirm the words of this law by doing them."

— Deuteronomy 27:26 (quoted in Galatians 3:10)

The curse is not arbitrary punishment. It is the lawful outcome of violating a righteous standard. To break God's revealed will is to stand under judgment—not because God is harsh, but because He is just.

Guilt under the Law is objective, not merely emotional. It is not the feeling of shame; it is the reality of standing accountable before a holy God. This is why attempts to silence guilt without addressing justice fail. Guilt persists because justice has not yet been answered.

"The wages of sin is death." — **Romans 6:23**

Reflection:

How does understanding guilt as objective accountability (not just emotion) change the way we view forgiveness?

Why Justice Must Be Satisfied

A central biblical truth emerges at this point: justice cannot be bypassed without destroying righteousness. God does not save by pretending sin does not matter. He saves by satisfying justice.

"He will by no means clear the guilty."
— **Exodus 34:7**

If God were to simply dismiss transgression, He would deny His own holiness. Forgiveness without justice would be moral contradiction. This is why Scripture insists that judgment under the Law is real—and why salvation must answer the Law's charge, not ignore it.

Paul explains God's purpose clearly:

"It was to show his righteousness… so that he might be just and the justifier of the one who has faith in Jesus."
— **Romans 3:26**

God remains just while justifying sinners because justice is satisfied, not dismissed. The Law demands a verdict; the gospel provides a fulfillment.

Reflection:

Why is a salvation that satisfies justice more trustworthy than one that ignores it?

Why This Prepares the Way for Christ

Understanding the Law's charge and condemnation prevents shallow views of grace. Grace is not leniency; it is costly fulfillment. Christ does not silence the Law; He answers it.

"Christ redeemed us from the curse of the law by becoming a curse for us." — **Galatians 3:13**

Only after the seriousness of transgression and judgment is understood can the depth of salvation be rightly grasped. The cross is not sentimental—it is judicial, redemptive, and victorious.

Chapter Summary

- The Law functions as witness and judge

- Transgression carries real charge and condemnation

- Guilt under the Law is objective accountability

- Justice must be satisfied, not ignored

- Christ fulfills the Law's demand and removes the curse

Final Reflection:

If justice must be satisfied for forgiveness to be true, how does the cross reveal both the seriousness of sin and the greatness of God's grace?

End of Chapter 8

CHAPTER 9

The Limits Of The Law

Scripture speaks of the Law with deep reverence—calling it holy, righteous, and good—yet it speaks with equal clarity about its limits. To understand salvation rightly, we must honor the Law for what God designed it to do and refuse to demand from it what God never intended it to accomplish.

"If a law had been given that could give life, then righteousness would indeed be by the law."
— Galatians 3:21

This chapter clarifies why obedience cannot produce life, why restraint is not transformation, and why the Law's limitation is not a flaw but a holy boundary set by God.

Why Obedience Cannot Produce Life

Obedience is often mistaken for life. Scripture never makes this mistake.

The Law commands righteousness, but it does not create it. It can instruct the will, but it cannot regenerate the heart.

Obedience under the Law can align behavior temporarily, but it cannot restore the life lost through sin.

Paul states this plainly:

"The very commandment that promised life proved to be death to me."

— Romans 7:10

The problem is not the commandment; the problem is the human condition. The Law speaks to a heart already affected by sin. It tells humanity what righteousness looks like, but it cannot supply the power to become righteous.

Life comes from God alone:

"It is the Spirit who gives life; the flesh is no help at all."

—John 6:63

Reflection:

Why does Scripture insist that life must be given, not achieved?

Why Restraint Is Not Transformation

The Law can restrain behavior. It can curb outward expressions of sin. But restraint is not the same as transformation.

A restrained heart may still desire what is forbidden. A disciplined life may still be inwardly misaligned. Scripture exposes this tension:

"The law is spiritual, but I am of the flesh, sold under sin."
— **Romans 7:14**

Restraint operates from the outside in; transformation operates from the inside out. The Law can say "do not," but it cannot create new desire. It can prohibit coveting, but it cannot produce love.

This is why God promises something greater than law-keeping:

"I will give you a new heart, and a new spirit I will put within you."
— **Ezekiel 36:26**

Transformation requires new creation, not stronger regulation.

Reflection:

Where have you experienced the difference between outward restraint and inward change?

The Law's Holy Purpose and Holy Limitation

Scripture never diminishes the Law's holiness—even as it draws a firm line around its function.

"So the law is holy, and the commandment is holy and righteous and good."

— Romans 7:12

The Law's holiness lies in its ability to:

- Reveal God's righteousness

- Expose sin and transgression

- Clarify guilt and accountability

- Prepare the way for salvation

Its limitation lies in what it cannot do:

- It cannot forgive sin

- It cannot heal the heart

- It cannot restore life

- It cannot reconcile humanity to God

This limitation is intentional. By defining the Law's boundary, God protects the gospel from distortion. The Law brings humanity to the end of self-reliance so that salvation may be received as gift, not earned as wage.

"The law was our guardian to bring us to Christ."
— Galatians 3:24

Reflection:

How does recognizing the Law's limitation deepen gratitude rather than diminish obedience?

Why the Law Must Yield to Fulfillment

The Law does not disappear; it is fulfilled. Its demands are met, its justice satisfied, and its purpose completed in Christ.

"For Christ is the end of the law for righteousness to everyone who believes."
— Romans 10:4

This does not mean the Law was wrong. It means the Law reached its intended goal. What the Law could not do—give life—God has done through His Son.

"For what the law could not do… God has done by sending his own Son." **— Romans 8:3**

Chapter Summary

- Obedience cannot produce life

- Restraint is not transformation

- The Law is holy in purpose and limited by design

- The Law prepares the way for Christ

- Life and righteousness come through salvation, not regulation

Final Reflection:

If the Law reveals righteousness but cannot produce life, how does this shape the way you understand grace, obedience, and transformation in Christ?

End of Chapter 9

PART III

Two Realities: Sin And Transgression

Introduction to Part III

By this point in Scripture's story, one truth is unmistakable: sin and transgression are related, but they are not the same. Confusing them leads either to despair or to false confidence. Separating them completely leads either to lawlessness or denial of accountability. Scripture does neither.

Part III holds these two realities together with biblical precision. Sin names the condition of misalignment with God—relational, ontological, and deadly. Transgression names the legal violation of a revealed command—chargeable, condemnable, and judicial. One explains why humanity is broken; the other explains why justice must be satisfied.

This section answers crucial questions:

- What is the charge of sin apart from law?

- Can a person be sinful without transgressing?

- How and when do sin and transgression converge?

- Why do fear and accusation persist—even among religious people?

- How is the Law misused when Christ is misunderstood?

Understanding these distinctions is essential for clarity about guilt, grace, assurance, and freedom in Christ.

Chapter 10 — The Charge of Sin

Sin carries a charge even where no law has been violated—because sin is first a relational rupture with God, not merely a legal infraction.

"Your iniquities have made a separation between you and your God."

— Isaiah 59:2

The charge of sin is not primarily courtroom guilt; it is separation, corruption, and death. Scripture presents death not merely as a penalty imposed from outside, but as the natural consequence of life disconnected from its source.

"The wages of sin is death."

— Romans 6:23

This chapter explains sin as a condition that corrupts the heart, distorts desire, and results in death—not simply as punishment, but as consequence.

Reflection:

How does viewing death as consequence rather than mere penalty change your understanding of God's justice?

Chapter 11 — Sin Without Transgression

Scripture clearly teaches that a person can be sinful without committing transgression—that is, misaligned with God without violating a known command.

"Sin indeed was in the world before the law was given."
— Romans 5:13

Before Sinai, humanity sinned, suffered death, and stood accountable to God—without Torah. This chapter explores biblical examples of sin without transgression, including ignorance, weakness, and inward misalignment.

Conscience convicts not because law has spoken, but because humanity remains morally aware—even when that awareness is incomplete or distorted.

Reflection:

Why does Scripture hold people accountable for sin even when they lack explicit commandments?

Chapter 12 — When Sin and Transgression Converge

The most serious condition Scripture describes is not sin alone or transgression alone, but their convergence.

"Whoever knows the right thing to do and fails to do it, for him it is sin."
— James 4:17

When the heart is misaligned, the will is informed, and action crosses a revealed boundary, sin becomes transgression. In this convergence, guilt is both relational and legal—the person is broken and guilty at the same time.

This chapter examines scriptural patterns where knowledge, desire, and action meet—showing why justice must be satisfied and why healing must also occur.

Reflection:

Why must salvation address both brokenness and guilt when sin and transgression converge?

Chapter 13 — Accusation, Fear, and False Assurance

When the Law is misunderstood or misused, it becomes a weapon rather than a witness. Accusation replaces conviction; fear replaces repentance; false assurance replaces true freedom.

"There is therefore now no condemnation for those who are in Christ Jesus."

— Romans 8:1

This chapter exposes how fear persists when Christ's fulfillment of the Law is not understood. It distinguishes conviction (which leads to life) from condemnation (which leads to despair), and explains how both legalism and lawlessness distort assurance.

Reflection:

How can misunderstanding the Law produce fear even in people who believe in grace?

Why Part III Matters

Part III protects the gospel from distortion by clarifying what Scripture actually teaches:

- *Sin explains why humanity is broken.*

- *Transgression explains why justice must be satisfied.*

- *Christ answers both.*

Only when these realities are rightly understood can assurance rest on Christ rather than on fear, performance, or denial.

CHAPTER 10

The Charge Of Sin

When Scripture speaks of the charge of sin, it is not first speaking in courtroom language, but in relational and existential terms. Sin carries a charge even where no written law has been violated, because sin is fundamentally a rupture with God—the Source of life, truth, and goodness.

The Law will later clarify guilt and pronounce condemnation where commands are broken. But before law, sin already carried consequences—real, devastating, and universal. Scripture names those consequences clearly: separation, corruption, and death.

Separation from God

The primary charge of sin is separation from God. This separation is not merely emotional distance; it is a relational breach that affects the entire human condition.

"Your iniquities have made a separation between you and your God."

— Isaiah 59:2

From the beginning, sin disrupts communion. Adam and Eve hide. Cain is driven away. Humanity is described as estranged. Separation is not imposed arbitrarily; it is the inevitable result of misalignment with a holy God.

Scripture describes humanity apart from God as:

- Alienated (Ephesians 4:18)

- Enemies in mind (Colossians 1:21)

- Without life (Ephesians 2:1)

This separation explains why humanity experiences restlessness, guilt, fear, and loss even apart from explicit commandments. Sin fractures relationship before it ever violates statute.

Reflection:

How does understanding sin as separation—rather than mere disobedience—reshape the way you think about reconciliation?

Corruption of the Heart

Sin does not remain external. Once relationship with God is fractured, the inner life becomes distorted. Scripture speaks of sin as corruption—affecting desire, thought, will, and affection.

"The heart is deceitful above all things, and desperately sick."

— Jeremiah 17:9

This corruption explains why humanity does not merely do wrong, but often desires what is wrong. Sin alters orientation. What once aligned with God now turns inward, producing self-rule, pride, and distorted love.

Paul describes this inward decay clearly:

"They became futile in their thinking, and their foolish hearts were darkened."

— Romans 1:21

The charge of sin, therefore, is not simply "you broke a rule," but "your heart has been turned from life." This is why moral improvement alone cannot solve the problem. Corruption requires renewal, not regulation.

Reflection:

Why is addressing behavior alone insufficient if the heart itself is corrupted?

Death as Consequence, Not Mere Penalty

Scripture is unambiguous: sin results in death. But death is not presented merely as a judicial penalty imposed from outside; it is the natural consequence of separation from the Source of life.

"The wages of sin is death." — **Romans 6:23**

From the beginning, God warns Adam that turning from Him results in death—not because God withdraws life arbitrarily, but because life cannot exist apart from Him.

"In the day that you eat of it you shall surely die."
— **Genesis 2:17**

This death unfolds in stages:

- Spiritual death — separation from God

- Moral death — corruption of desire and will

- Physical death — the body's return to dust

Death reigns wherever sin reigns, even before law:

"Death reigned from Adam to Moses."
— **Romans 5:14**

This confirms that death is not merely a legal sentence—it is the inevitable outcome of life disconnected from God.

Reflection:

How does viewing death as consequence rather than arbitrary punishment affect your understanding of God's justice?

Why the Charge of Sin Requires Salvation

The charge of sin—separation, corruption, and death—cannot be answered by law, discipline, or effort. Law can clarify guilt; it cannot restore life. Healing this condition requires reconciliation, renewal, and resurrection life.

"For as in Adam all die, so also in Christ shall all be made alive."
— 1 Corinthians 15:22

Salvation is God's answer to the charge of sin. It restores relationship, renews the heart, and overcomes death—not by denying the seriousness of sin, but by addressing it fully in Christ.

Chapter Summary

- The charge of sin is separation from God

- Sin corrupts the heart, not just behavior

- Death is the consequence of misalignment with God

- Sin carries real effects even without written law

- Salvation must restore life, not merely remove guilt

Final Reflection:

If sin results in separation, corruption, and death, what must salvation accomplish for life to be truly restored?

End of Chapter 10

CHAPTER 11

Sin Without Transgression

Scripture makes room for a reality that is often overlooked or misunderstood: a person can be sinful without committing transgression. That is, a person can live in misalignment with God without violating a known, revealed command. This distinction is not a theological loophole—it is a biblical necessity if we are to understand humanity's condition before the Law, and even beyond it.

"Sin indeed was in the world before the law was given."
— **Romans 5:13**

Sin existed, death reigned, and humanity stood accountable to God—without Torah. This chapter explores how Scripture presents sin apart from transgression, why ignorance and weakness matter without excusing sin, and why conscience convicts even when no command has been cited.

Biblical Examples of Sin Without Transgression

Scripture provides multiple examples where sin is present and consequential even though no explicit command has been violated.

Adam (before Torah):

Adam's disobedience occurs before any codified law exists. While God gave a direct word, there was no legal system, no covenantal code, and no judicial structure like Sinai. Yet sin entered, relationship was broken, and death followed (Genesis 3).

The generations before the Flood:

God judges the world not for violating statutes, but for pervasive wickedness and corruption of the heart.

"Every intention of the thoughts of his heart was only evil continually."
— Genesis 6:5

The nations (Gentiles):

Paul speaks of people who did not possess the Law yet were still accountable.

"When Gentiles, who do not have the law, by nature do what the law requires…"
— Romans 2:14

These examples confirm that sin is not dependent on possessing written law. Accountability exists because relationship with God exists.

Reflection:

Why does Scripture consistently hold people accountable even where no formal law code is present?

Ignorance, Weakness, and Inner Misalignment

Scripture does not treat ignorance as innocence, but neither does it treat ignorance as identical to willful rebellion. There is a difference between not knowing, being weak, and knowingly transgressing—yet all can still fall under sin.

Paul acknowledges this complexity:

"I obtained mercy because I had acted ignorantly in unbelief." — **1 Timothy 1:13**

Ignorance mitigates culpability, but it does not erase the condition. A person may not know God's revealed will, yet still live in misalignment with God's truth and life.

Weakness likewise does not eliminate sin. Scripture describes humanity as unable to fulfill righteousness apart from God's intervention:

"For we do not have a high priest who is unable to sympathize with our weaknesses." — **Hebrews 4:15**

Inner misalignment—desire turned inward, will disconnected from God—exists even where no explicit rule is broken. This is why salvation must heal the heart, not merely correct actions.

Reflection:

How does Scripture balance mercy toward ignorance with truth about sin's seriousness?

Why Conscience Convicts Without Law

Even without written law, humans often experience conviction—an inner sense that something is wrong. Scripture explains this phenomenon carefully, without elevating conscience to moral authority.

"Their conscience also bears witness, and their conflicting thoughts accuse or even excuse them."
— Romans 2:15

Conscience convicts because humans are moral beings created accountable to God. Yet conscience is not infallible. It is shaped by culture, environment, habit, and revelation. This is why Scripture speaks of consciences that are weak, defiled, or seared.

Conscience explains why people feel accountable without law. It does not define what is truly right or wrong. That authority belongs to God's revealed truth.

Reflection:

Why is it dangerous to rely on conscience alone to define righteousness?

Why This Distinction Matters

Understanding sin without transgression guards against two serious errors:

- Legalism, which assumes sin only exists where rules are broken

- Moral relativism, which assumes ignorance removes accountability

Scripture rejects both. Sin explains the human condition; transgression explains legal guilt. One reveals the need for healing; the other reveals the need for justice satisfied.

"All have sinned and fall short of the glory of God."

— Romans 3:23

Chapter Summary

- Sin can exist without transgression

- Biblical history shows accountability before written law

- Ignorance and weakness affect culpability, not the condition

- Conscience bears witness but does not define truth

- Salvation must address misalignment, not just rule-breaking

Final Reflection:

If a person can be sinful without transgressing a known command, what does that reveal about humanity's deepest need—and why must salvation go beyond law?

End of Chapter 11

CHAPTER 12

When Sin And Transgression Converge

Scripture does not treat sin and transgression as mutually exclusive realities. While they can exist separately, the most serious condition occurs when they converge—when inner misalignment meets revealed truth and results in deliberate action. In this convergence, a person is not only broken (sinful in condition) but also guilty (answerable for violating known command).

This chapter traces how heart, knowledge, and action come together, why Scripture holds people fully accountable in such moments, and how these patterns appear consistently throughout the biblical record.

Heart, Knowledge, and Action

The convergence of sin and transgression follows a recognizable biblical pattern:

1. The heart is already misaligned (desire, pride, fear, self-rule).

2. Knowledge of God's will is present—truth has been revealed.

3. Action crosses a known boundary.

Scripture describes this progression plainly:

"Each person is tempted when he is lured and enticed by his own desire. Then desire when it has conceived gives birth to sin, and sin when it is fully grown brings forth death."
— **James 1:14–15**

Desire alone is not yet transgression. Knowledge alone does not condemn. But when desire acts against known truth, sin becomes transgression—and accountability becomes both relational and legal.

Another clear statement captures this convergence:

"Whoever knows the right thing to do and fails to do it, for him it is sin." — **James 4:17**

Here, knowledge transforms inward failure into chargeable guilt.

Reflection:

Why does Scripture place such weight on knowing and then acting against truth?

Why People Can Be Both Broken and Guilty

Scripture refuses to choose between compassion and accountability. A person can be broken by sin and guilty of transgression at the same time. Brokenness explains the condition; guilt explains responsibility.

Paul describes this tension in his own experience:

"I do not do the good I want, but the evil I do not want is what I keep on doing."

— Romans 7:19

Paul acknowledges inner corruption—

yet never uses it to excuse responsibility.

Scripture holds together two truths:

- Humanity is affected by sin and weakness

- Humanity remains accountable for choices made in the light of truth

This balance prevents despair ("I am only broken") and denial ("I am only guilty"). Salvation must therefore heal the broken heart and satisfy justice for guilt.

Reflection:

How does holding brokenness and guilt together protect the gospel from distortion?

Scriptural Patterns of Convergence

Scripture repeatedly presents moments where sin and transgression converge:

David (2 Samuel 11–12):

David's desire, knowledge of God's law, and deliberate action converge. His sin is both inward corruption and explicit transgression. David does not deny guilt; he confesses it.

"Against you, you only, have I sinned."

— Psalm 51:4

Israel under the Law:

Israel repeatedly sins after receiving clear revelation. Their guilt is intensified not because God is harsher, but because knowledge has increased.

"You only have I known of all the families of the earth; therefore I will punish you for all your iniquities."

— Amos 3:2

The New Testament warning:

The apostles consistently warn believers not to treat grace as immunity from responsibility.

"How shall we escape if we neglect such a great salvation?"
— **Hebrews 2:3**

These patterns show that convergence is not accidental;
it is the predictable result of light meeting resistance.

Reflection:

Why does Scripture increase warning where revelation is greatest?

Why Convergence Demands Both Justice and Healing

When sin and transgression converge, neither denial nor discipline alone can resolve the problem. Justice must be satisfied because guilt is real. Healing must occur because the heart is broken.

This is why the gospel centers on Christ, not on law or effort.

"For our sake he made him to be sin who knew no sin, so that in him we might become the righteousness of God."

— **2 Corinthians 5:21**

Christ answers the convergence:

- He satisfies justice for transgression

- He restores life to the broken heart

Only in Him can guilt be removed without denying truth, and healing occur without dismissing responsibility.

Chapter Summary

- Sin and transgression converge when heart, knowledge, and action align against God

- People can be both broken and guilty at the same time

- Scripture consistently presents moments of convergence

- Increased revelation increases accountability

- Salvation must address both justice and healing

Final Reflection:

If sin and transgression converge where truth is known and resisted, how does Christ's work free us from both guilt and despair?

End of Chapter 12

CHAPTER 13

Accusation, Fear, And False Assurance

When the Law is misunderstood, it becomes something Scripture never intended it to be: a weapon. Instead of serving as a witness to truth and a tutor leading to Christ, the Law is misused to accuse, intimidate, and produce fear. Where Christ is not clearly understood, accusation replaces conviction, fear replaces repentance, and false assurance replaces true peace.

This chapter exposes how these distortions arise and why only a right understanding of Christ brings freedom.

Law Misused as a Weapon

The Law was given to reveal truth, not to destroy hope. Yet Scripture warns that when the Law is separated from its fulfillment in Christ, it can be wielded to condemn rather than to lead to life.

Paul names the result plainly:

"The letter kills, but the Spirit gives life."

— 2 Corinthians 3:6

When the Law is used as a weapon:

- It is applied without mercy

- It focuses on exposure without offering restoration

- It produces fear rather than repentance

This misuse often mirrors the work of the accuser:

"The accuser of our brothers… who accuses them day and night before our God."
— Revelation 12:10

The Law, when divorced from Christ, becomes a voice of relentless accusation. But Scripture never presents accusation as God's final word to His people.

Reflection:

How can truth meant to lead us to Christ become a tool of fear when Christ is removed from the center?

Conviction vs. Condemnation

Scripture draws a sharp line between conviction and condemnation—a distinction essential for assurance.

- Conviction exposes sin in order to heal

- Condemnation pronounces guilt in order to destroy

Conviction comes from the Spirit and leads to repentance and life:

"When he comes, he will convict the world concerning sin and righteousness and judgment." **— John 16:8**

Condemnation, by contrast, leaves no path forward. It tells the sinner not only what is wrong, but that there is no hope. Scripture explicitly denies condemnation to those in Christ:

"There is therefore now no condemnation for those who are in Christ Jesus." **— Romans 8:1**

Where condemnation reigns, Christ's finished work is either misunderstood or ignored.

Reflection:

How does the presence—or absence—of hope reveal whether a message is conviction or condemnation?

Why Fear Persists Without Understanding Christ

Fear persists where the Law's demands are felt but Christ's fulfillment is not trusted. People may believe in God, acknowledge sin, and even strive for obedience—yet still live in fear because justice feels unresolved.

Scripture explains this dynamic:

"Perfect love casts out fear, for fear has to do with punishment."

— 1 John 4:18

Fear remains when punishment is still expected. This is why partial understanding of the gospel produces unstable assurance. Where Christ is seen as helper rather than fulfillment, fear lingers.

True assurance rests not on performance, but on Christ's completed work:

"By a single offering he has perfected for all time those who are being sanctified."

— Hebrews 10:14

Without this clarity, people oscillate between self-effort and despair—never fully at rest.

Reflection:

What fears remain when Christ is seen as assistance rather than as fulfillment?

False Assurance: The Other Extreme

Fear is not the only danger. Where the Law is dismissed entirely, false assurance emerges. Scripture warns against confidence that ignores repentance, truth, and transformation.

"Shall we continue in sin that grace may abound? By no means!"

— Romans 6:1–2

False assurance treats grace as permission and dismisses conviction altogether. It silences conscience, ignores Scripture, and mistakes God's patience for approval.

True assurance is neither fearful nor careless. It rests on Christ while producing a transformed life.

Reflection:

Why is assurance without transformation just as dangerous as fear without grace?

Christ: The End of Accusation and the Ground of Assurance

Christ does not silence the Law; He fulfills it. He does not deny justice; He satisfies it. This is why accusation loses its power in Him.

"Who shall bring any charge against God's elect? It is God who justifies."
— Romans 8:33

In Christ:

- Accusation is answered

- Fear is displaced by love

- Assurance rests on finished work

The gospel does not produce careless confidence
or crippling fear.
It produces peace with God.

"Since we have been justified by faith, we have peace with God through our Lord Jesus Christ."
— Romans 5:1

Chapter Summary

- The Law can be misused as a weapon when separated from Christ

- Conviction leads to life; condemnation leads to fear

- Fear persists when justice feels unresolved

- False assurance ignores conviction and transformation

- True assurance rests on Christ's fulfilled work

Final Reflection:

If Christ has fully satisfied justice, what accusations or fears are you still carrying—and why?

End of Chapter 13

PART IV

Christ And The Fulfillment Of The Law

Introduction to Part IV

Everything Scripture has revealed up to this point leads to one unavoidable conclusion: the Law was never meant to be the final object of faith. It was given by God, holy and true, but it was always on the way to Someone greater.

The Law reveals God's righteousness.

The Law exposes sin and defines transgression.

The Law demands justice.

But the Law cannot give life.

This is where Jesus Christ stands at the center of redemptive history—not as a revision to the Law, but as its completion. Christ does not compete with the Law; He finishes what the Law began. He fulfills its righteousness, satisfies its justice, and accomplishes what no human obedience ever could.

"For Christ is the end of the law for righteousness to everyone who believes." **— Romans 10:4**

Because Christ fulfills the Law perfectly, faith must now move. Those who once relied on the Law are called to place their trust wholly in Christ—not in commands, performance, or fear, but in His finished work and living presence.

Part IV marks this decisive transition:

- From Law as tutor → Christ as Lord

- From external regulation → internal life

- From fear-driven obedience → Spirit-formed obedience

- From righteousness pursued → righteousness received

Here, salvation is seen not as escape from the Law, but as the Law's rightful fulfillment in Christ.

Chapter 14 — Christ Did Not Abolish the Law

Jesus directly addresses the question that stands at the heart of this book:

"Do not think that I have come to abolish the Law or the Prophets; I have not come to abolish them but to fulfill them."

— Matthew 5:17

Christ did not cancel the Law, silence it, or dismiss its authority. He fulfilled it—bringing it to its intended goal. Fulfillment means the Law's purpose is completed, not discarded.

In Christ:

- The Law's righteousness is embodied

- The Law's demands are satisfied

- The Law's testimony is confirmed

This chapter establishes that the Law remains honored, not ignored—but no longer stands as the way of righteousness. That role belongs to Christ alone.

Chapter 15 — How Christ Answers the Charge of Transgression

Transgression creates legal guilt. The Law bears witness, records the offense, and pronounces condemnation. Scripture never denies this—but it declares that Christ answers it fully and finally.

"By canceling the record of debt that stood against us with its legal demands… he set it aside, nailing it to the cross."

— Colossians 2:14

Christ does not argue with the Law; He satisfies it. Justice is not bypassed—it is fulfilled. The record is not hidden—it is canceled.

— Romans 8:1

This chapter shows how condemnation ends because justice is answered, not because guilt is denied.

Chapter 16 — How Christ Heals the Charge of Sin

The charge of sin is deeper than legal guilt. Sin brings separation, corruption, and death. Forgiveness alone cannot heal this condition—life must be restored.

"If anyone is in Christ, he is a new creation."
— 2 Corinthians 5:17

Christ does not merely remove penalty; He restores relationship. He does not merely forgive; He recreates. Where death reigned through Adam, life now reigns through Christ.

"For as in Adam all die, so also in Christ shall all be made alive." **— 1 Corinthians 15:22**

This chapter presents salvation as healing, renewal, and restored life—not merely acquittal.

Chapter 17 — From External Law to Internal Life

The Law spoke from the outside, commanding what the heart could not fulfill. Christ brings life from within through the Spirit.

"I will put my law within them, and I will write it on their hearts." — **Jeremiah 31:33**

In Christ, obedience flows from new life, not fear. The Spirit transforms desire so that righteousness becomes fruit, not pressure.

"Walk by the Spirit, and you will not gratify the desires of the flesh."
— **Galatians 5:16**

This chapter clarifies what it means to follow Jesus—not as law-keeping under a new name, but as Spirit-empowered life shaped by union with Christ.

Why Part IV Is the Turning Point

Part IV proclaims the heart of the gospel with clarity:

- The Law reveals.

- Christ fulfills.

- Justice is satisfied.

- Life is restored.

The Law leads to Christ.

But Christ—not the Law—is the way, the truth, and the life.

"I am the way, and the truth, and the life."
— John 14:6

CHAPTER 14

Christ Did Not Abolish The Law

Jesus' words about the Law are not a defense of legalism nor a denial of grace. They are a revelation of transition—from Law to Christ as the object of faith.

"Do not think that I have come to abolish the Law or the Prophets; I have not come to abolish them but to fulfill them."
— Matthew 5:17

To fulfill the Law is not to preserve it as the path of righteousness, but to complete its purpose so that faith may move where the Law always pointed.

Fulfillment, Not Cancellation

If Jesus had abolished the Law, He would have denied its truth. If He had merely preserved it, humanity would remain trapped under a standard no one can meet. Instead, He fulfills it—bringing it to its intended end.

Fulfillment means:

- The Law's testimony is confirmed

- The Law's demands are met

- The Law's goal is reached

The Law never claimed to be the way of life. It claimed to be the witness to righteousness. That witness now stands complete in Christ.

"The law was our guardian to bring us to Christ, that we might be justified by faith."
— Galatians 3:24

A tutor is honored by finishing its task—not by being clung to after the goal is reached.

Reflection:

If the Law was meant to lead you to Christ, what happens when faith stops at the Law instead of moving forward?

Law Satisfied, Not Ignored

Grace does not pretend the Law never spoke. The Law spoke truthfully—and it demanded justice. Christ does not dispute that demand; He satisfies it.

"For what the law could not do, weakened by the flesh, God did by sending his own Son."

— Romans 8:3

The Law could expose sin but could not remove it. It could pronounce guilt but could not restore life. Christ answers both.

"Christ redeemed us from the curse of the law by becoming a curse for us."

— Galatians 3:13

Justice is not dismissed; it is fulfilled. Condemnation ends not because standards are lowered, but because righteousness has been fully accomplished.

Reflection:

How does knowing that justice is satisfied—not suspended—free you from fear?

Christ as the Law's Completion (and the New Object of Faith)

Here is the decisive shift Scripture demands:

"For Christ is the end of the law for righteousness to everyone who believes." **— Romans 10:4**

"End" means goal, completion, arrival. The Law's role as the path to righteousness ends because righteousness has arrived—in a Person.

This means something crucial and unavoidable:

- No one fulfills the Law but Christ

- Therefore, no one can place faith in the Law

- Faith must now be placed in Christ Himself

To continue trusting the Law after Christ has fulfilled it is not obedience—it is refusal to move where the Law points.

"You search the Scriptures because you think that in them you have eternal life; and it is they that bear witness about me."

— John 5:39

Scripture bears witness. Christ gives life.

Reflection:

Where do you still look for righteousness— standards you try to meet, or the Savior who has met them?

From Following the Law to Following Jesus

Because Christ fulfills the Law, the center of faith shifts:

- From commands → to Christ

- From performance → to trust

- From fear → to relationship

This is not lawlessness. It is new-covenant obedience—obedience that flows from union with Christ rather than pressure to earn acceptance.

"The life I now live in the flesh I live by faith in the Son of God."
— Galatians 2:20

Those who once followed the Law are now called to follow Jesus—to trust Him, walk with Him, and live from His life.

Why This Matters for Salvation

If Christ fulfills the Law, then:

- Righteousness is received, not achieved

- Obedience is fruit, not currency

- Assurance rests on Christ's work, not ours

"There is therefore now no condemnation for those who are in Christ Jesus."

— Romans 8:1

Condemnation ends because the Law's work is finished in Christ—and faith now rests where life truly is.

Chapter Summary

- Christ did not abolish the Law; He fulfilled it

- Fulfillment completes the Law's purpose and ends it as a path to righteousness

- Justice is satisfied, not ignored

- Faith moves from the Law to Christ

- Following Jesus replaces trusting the Law as the way of life

Final Reflection:

If Christ has fulfilled what you never could, what would it look like to stop striving under the Law and begin fully trusting—and following—Him?

End of Chapter 14

CHAPTER 15

How Christ Answers The Charge Of Transgression

Transgression creates a legal charge. When God's revealed command is violated, guilt is not merely felt—it is established. The Law bears witness, records the offense, and demands justice. Scripture never minimizes this reality. Instead, it proclaims something greater: Christ answers the charge fully and finally.

This chapter shows how justice is satisfied, how the record of debt is canceled, and why condemnation ends—not by denial of guilt, but by fulfillment of justice in Christ.

Justice Satisfied

Justice is not an obstacle to salvation; it is a requirement of God's righteousness. If God were to overlook transgression without satisfaction, He would deny His own holiness. The gospel does not weaken justice—it fulfills it.

"It was to show his righteousness... so that he might be just and the justifier of the one who has faith in Jesus."

— Romans 3:26

At the cross, Christ does not argue innocence for the guilty. He bears the judgment that the Law rightly pronounces.

"Christ redeemed us from the curse of the law by becoming a curse for us." — **Galatians 3:13**

Justice is satisfied because the penalty demanded by the Law is paid—not symbolically, not partially, but completely. This is why salvation is secure: it rests on satisfied justice, not suspended judgment.

Reflection:

Why is a salvation that satisfies justice more trustworthy than one that simply overlooks guilt?

The Record of Debt Canceled

Transgression leaves a record. Scripture speaks of a written account—charges standing against us with legal force. The gospel does not pretend this record never existed. It proclaims that it has been canceled.

"By canceling the record of debt that stood against us with its legal demands. This he set aside, nailing it to the cross." — **Colossians 2:14**

The language is deliberate and judicial. The record is not hidden, reduced, or postponed. It is set aside because it has been fully answered. The Law's demands are met in Christ's death.

This is why Scripture can say:

"Who shall bring any charge against God's elect? It is God who justifies." — **Romans 8:33**

No charge remains because no unpaid debt remains.

Reflection:

If the record of debt is canceled, what accusations do you still carry that Scripture says no longer stand?

No Condemnation in Christ

Because justice is satisfied and the record is canceled, the verdict changes—not because truth is ignored, but because it is fulfilled.

"There is therefore now no condemnation for those who are in Christ Jesus." — **Romans 8:1**

"No condemnation" does not mean "no accountability." It means the charge has been answered. Condemnation ends because the Law's rightful demand has been met in Christ.

Scripture emphasizes the finality of this work:

"By a single offering he has perfected for all time those who are being sanctified."

— Hebrews 10:14

Perfection here refers to standing before God—not to moral flawlessness, but to completed justification. The believer's status is secure because Christ's work is complete.

Reflection:

How does "no condemnation" change the way you relate to God in moments of failure or weakness?

Why This Ends Fear and Accusation

Fear persists where justice feels unresolved. Accusation thrives where guilt still seems unpaid. But where Christ's satisfaction is understood, fear loses its ground.

"Perfect love casts out fear, for fear has to do with punishment." **— 1 John 4:18**

The gospel does not silence the Law by force; it answers it by love expressed through justice fulfilled. This is why assurance is not denial—it is confidence in Christ.

Chapter Summary

- Transgression creates a real legal charge

- Christ satisfies justice on behalf of sinners

- The record of debt is fully canceled at the cross

- Condemnation ends because justice is fulfilled

- Assurance rests on Christ's finished work, not human performance

Final Reflection:

If Christ has fully answered every charge against you, what would it look like to live without fear—trusting not in yourself, but in His finished work?

End of Chapter 15

CHAPTER 16

How Christ Heals The Charge Of Sin

If transgression answers to justice, sin answers to life. The charge of sin is deeper than legal guilt—it is separation from God, corruption of the heart, and the reign of death. Forgiveness alone cannot heal this condition. What is required is new creation, restored relationship, and life where death once ruled.

Christ does not merely cancel the record; He restores the person.

New Creation

Sin damages humanity at the level of being, not just behavior. Therefore, salvation must do more than pardon—it must recreate.

"If anyone is in Christ, he is a new creation. The old has passed away; behold, the new has come."

— 2 Corinthians 5:17

New creation is not self-improvement. It is not moral repair. It is God's creative act—bringing life where death had authority. The old identity shaped by sin is not rehabilitated; it is replaced by life in Christ.

This is why Scripture speaks of being "born again," not merely instructed or corrected.

"That which is born of the flesh is flesh, and that which is born of the Spirit is spirit."
— John 3:6

Reflection:

Why does Scripture insist on new birth rather than better behavior as the answer to sin?

Restored Relationship

Sin's primary charge is separation. Christ's healing work restores communion with God, not merely peace of conscience.

"While we were enemies we were reconciled to God by the death of his Son."
— Romans 5:10

Reconciliation is relational, not symbolic. Hostility ends. Distance is removed. Access is restored.

"For through him we both have access in one Spirit to the Father."

— Ephesians 2:18

This restored relationship answers the deepest wound of sin: alienation from God. Salvation is not merely rescue from punishment—it is return to fellowship.

Reflection:

How does reconciliation with God change the way you understand salvation beyond forgiveness?

Life Where Death Once Reigned

Sin brought death—not only physical death, but spiritual separation and moral decay. Christ reverses this reign by imparting His own life.

"For as in Adam all die, so also in Christ shall all be made alive."

— 1 Corinthians 15:22

Life in Christ is not postponed until the future. It begins now.

"Even when we were dead in our trespasses, [God] made us alive together with Christ."
— **Ephesians 2:5**

Where death once governed desire, identity, and destiny, Christ now reigns with life. This life expresses itself in renewed desire, growing holiness, and hope that reaches beyond the grave.

Reflection:

Where do you still live as if death reigns, rather than Christ's life?

Why Healing Completes Salvation

Justice answers guilt. Healing restores life. Salvation requires both.

If guilt were removed without healing, people would remain broken.

If healing were offered without justice, righteousness would be denied.

Christ does both:

- He satisfies the Law's demand for justice
- He restores the sinner to life and relationship

"I came that they may have life and have it abundantly."

— John 10:10

Chapter Summary

- Sin's charge is separation, corruption, and death
- Christ brings new creation, not mere repair
- Relationship with God is restored
- Life replaces death's reign
- Salvation heals what sin destroyed

Final Reflection:

If Christ has made you a new creation and restored you to God, what does it mean to live today from life rather than from fear or brokenness?

End of Chapter 16

CHAPTER 17

From External Law To Internal Life

The Law spoke from the outside, commanding righteousness it could not produce. Christ brings life from within, giving what the Law could only describe. This chapter marks the final movement of salvation's logic: from external regulation to internal transformation, from fear-driven compliance to Spirit-formed obedience, from striving under command to walking like Christ.

"I will put my law within them, and I will write it on their hearts." **— Jeremiah 31:33**

The Spirit's Work

What the Law could not do because of the weakness of the flesh, God does by giving His Spirit. The Spirit does not replace righteousness; He produces it.

"For the law of the Spirit of life has set you free in Christ Jesus from the law of sin and death."

— Romans 8:2

The Spirit's work is not external enforcement but internal renewal:

- A new heart replaces the old

- New desires replace old dominions

- New power replaces human weakness

"I will give you a new heart, and a new spirit I will put within you… and cause you to walk in my statutes."
— **Ezekiel 36:26–27**

This is not lawlessness; it is life empowered by God Himself.

Reflection:

Why is obedience that is caused by the Spirit fundamentally different from obedience demanded by law?

Obedience from Renewal, Not Fear

Fear-based obedience is the natural result of law without life. It restrains behavior but cannot transform desire. The gospel replaces fear with love, and compulsion with confidence.

"There is no fear in love, but perfect love casts out fear."
— **1 John 4:18**

Obedience under the new covenant flows from identity, not insecurity. The believer obeys not to become accepted, but because they are already accepted in Christ.

"Work out your own salvation with fear and trembling, for it is God who works in you."

— Philippians 2:12–13

God works within, and obedience emerges as fruit—not currency.

Reflection:

How does knowing that God works within you change the motivation behind obedience?

Walking Like Christ

Following Jesus does not mean imitating rules; it means sharing His life. The Spirit forms Christ's character in those who belong to Him.

"Whoever says he abides in him ought to walk in the same way in which he walked."

— 1 John 2:6

Walking like Christ is not perfectionism. It is direction—daily alignment with His life, love, and truth.

"It is no longer I who live, but Christ who lives in me."
— Galatians 2:20

This walk is sustained by:

- Abiding, not striving

- Faith, not fear

- Love, not law

Reflection:

What does it practically mean for Christ to live His life through you today?

Why Internal Life Is the Law's True Fulfillment

The Law's righteous requirement is not discarded—it is fulfilled in those who live by the Spirit.

"In order that the righteous requirement of the law might be fulfilled in us, who walk not according to the flesh but according to the Spirit." **— Romans 8:4**

This is the Law's final word: not command without power, but life with righteousness.

Chapter Summary

- The Spirit accomplishes what the Law could not

- Obedience flows from renewal, not fear

- Internal life replaces external regulation

- Walking like Christ means living from union with Him

- The Law's purpose is fulfilled through Spirit-empowered life

Final Reflection:

If obedience now flows from life within rather than pressure without, how would that change the way you walk with Christ each day?

End of Chapter 17

PART V

Salvation Alone: Life After The Law

Introduction to Part V

Part V brings the journey to its lived conclusion. If the Law has fulfilled its purpose in Christ—if justice has been satisfied, sin healed, and life restored—then the believer now stands in a new reality: life after the Law.

This is not lawlessness. It is salvation alone—a life grounded entirely in Christ's finished work and sustained by His living presence. Here, assurance replaces fear, holiness flows from grace, growth occurs without shame, and reconciliation becomes the daily experience of those who live in Christ.

"For freedom Christ has set us free; stand firm therefore, and do not submit again to a yoke of slavery."
— Galatians 5:1

Part V answers the practical question every reader eventually asks:

What does life look like when salvation—not the Law—is the foundation?

Chapter 18 — No Condemnation

When Christ satisfies justice and cancels the record of debt, condemnation no longer has a legal or spiritual claim. Assurance is not emotional optimism; it is grounded in Christ's finished work.

"There is therefore now no condemnation for those who are in Christ Jesus."

— Romans 8:1

This chapter establishes why salvation is secure—not because believers are flawless, but because Christ's work is complete. Freedom from fear of judgment is not denial of sin; it is confidence in fulfilled justice.

Key emphasis:

Assurance flows from Christ's accomplishment, not human consistency.

Chapter 19 — Holiness Without Legalism

Grace does not weaken holiness—it produces it. When the Law is no longer the means of acceptance, obedience becomes the fruit of transformation rather than the price of approval.

"For the grace of God has appeared… training us to renounce ungodliness." **— Titus 2:11–12**

This chapter shows how holiness flourishes without fear, how obedience emerges from love, and why love—not rule-keeping—is the fulfillment of God's will.

"Love is the fulfilling of the law."
— Romans 13:10

Key emphasis:

Obedience is fruit, not payment.

Chapter 20 — Living by the Spirit

Life after the Law is not guided by unchecked conscience or self-effort, but by a renewed conscience formed by truth and empowered by the Spirit.

"If we live by the Spirit, let us also keep in step with the Spirit."
— Galatians 5:25

This chapter addresses growth without shame, sanctification grounded in truth, and how the Spirit leads believers into increasing freedom and maturity without condemnation.

Key emphasis:

Sanctification is growth in life, not survival under pressure.

Chapter 21 — A Life Reconciled to God

Salvation's final picture is not merely forgiven sinners, but reconciled children—standing in peace with God, living from mercy, and restored to life in Christ.

"Since we have been justified by faith, we have peace with God through our Lord Jesus Christ."

— **Romans 5:1**

This chapter gathers everything together:

- Justice honored

- Mercy received

- Life restored

Salvation alone does not diminish righteousness—it completes it in Christ.

Key emphasis:

Reconciliation is the goal; life in Christ is the outcome.

Why Part V Matters

Part V answers the fear that remains when people leave the Law behind:

If not the Law, then what governs life?

Scripture's answer is clear:

- Christ governs life.
- The Spirit empowers obedience.
- Love fulfills righteousness.

Life after the Law is not emptiness—it is fullness.

CHAPTER 18

No Condemnation

The declaration "no condemnation" is not emotional reassurance; it is a judicial verdict grounded in Christ's finished work. Condemnation ends not because sin is denied, but because justice has been satisfied and the charge has been answered. Assurance, therefore, rests on what Christ has done—once and for all.

"There is therefore now no condemnation for those who are in Christ Jesus."

— Romans 8:1

This chapter explains why assurance is secure, why salvation cannot be undone by fear, and how freedom from judgment becomes the daily posture of life in Christ.

Assurance Grounded in Christ's Finished Work

Assurance does not come from inner confidence or consistent performance. It comes from a completed act outside of us—the cross and resurrection of Jesus Christ.

"By a single offering he has perfected for all time those who are being sanctified."

— Hebrews 10:14

"Perfected" speaks to standing before God, not sinless behavior. The believer's status is settled because Christ's offering is final. The Law's demands are met; the record of debt is canceled; the verdict has been rendered.

This is why assurance does not fluctuate with spiritual mood. It is anchored to history—to the once-for-all work of Christ.

Reflection:

If assurance depends on Christ's finished work rather than your present condition, what changes in the way you face failure?

Why Salvation Is Secure

Salvation is secure because it rests on God's action, not human effort. What God has justified, no accusation can overturn.

"Who shall bring any charge against God's elect? It is God who justifies."

— Romans 8:33

The courtroom language is intentional. Charges may be raised, memories may accuse, and conscience may tremble—but the verdict has already been issued by the highest authority.

Scripture grounds security not in perseverance of effort, but in the perseverance of Christ's intercession:

"He is able to save to the uttermost those who draw near to God through him."

— Hebrews 7:25

Salvation is secure because Christ lives, reigns, and intercedes. Fear cannot undo what resurrection has established.

Reflection:

What does it reveal about trust when security is sought in effort rather than in Christ's intercession?

Freedom from Fear of Judgment

Fear persists where judgment feels unresolved. But where condemnation has ended, fear loses its foundation.

"Perfect love casts out fear, for fear has to do with punishment." **— 1 John 4:18**

This does not mean believers never experience conviction. Conviction leads to repentance and restoration. Condemnation, however, declares there is no way back. Scripture explicitly removes condemnation for those in Christ.

"There is therefore now no condemnation…"

— **Romans 8:1**

The word "now" matters. Freedom from condemnation is not postponed to the final judgment—it is a present reality that shapes daily life. Believers approach God not as defendants awaiting sentence, but as children welcomed into grace.

Reflection:

How does living without fear of judgment change the way you approach God in prayer and obedience?

Assurance Without Carelessness

"No condemnation" is not permission to sin; it is freedom to live. Assurance does not weaken holiness—it strengthens it by removing fear and restoring trust.

"We love because he first loved us."

— **1 John 4:19**

When fear is removed, obedience flows from love rather than pressure. Growth happens in safety, not threat. This is the environment in which true transformation occurs.

Chapter Summary

- Condemnation ends because justice is fulfilled in Christ

- Assurance is grounded in Christ's finished work, not human performance

- Salvation is secure because God justifies and Christ intercedes

- Fear of judgment has no authority in Christ

- Freedom from condemnation produces trust, love, and growth

Final Reflection:

If condemnation no longer defines your standing before God, what would it look like to live today in the freedom Christ has already secured?

End of Chapter 18

CHAPTER 19

Holiness Without Legalism

Holiness is not abandoned when the Law no longer governs salvation. It is liberated. When righteousness is no longer pursued through fear, pressure, or performance, holiness becomes the fruit of grace, not the burden of law. Scripture never presents grace and holiness as opposites; it presents grace as the only power that can truly produce holiness.

"For the grace of God has appeared... training us to renounce ungodliness and worldly passions."
— **Titus 2:11–12**

This chapter shows how grace transforms the heart, why obedience flows as fruit rather than payment, and how love fulfills God's will without legalism.

Grace That Transforms

Grace is not God lowering His standards; it is God changing the person. Legalism tries to control behavior without transforming desire. Grace works from the inside out.

— Romans 6:14

Under the Law, sin is restrained but not defeated. Under grace, sin's dominion is broken. Grace does not merely forgive past failure; it reshapes present life.

This is why Scripture never treats grace as passive mercy. Grace trains, teaches, and forms the believer into holiness.

Reflection:

Why is inward transformation more powerful than external regulation in producing holiness?

Obedience as Fruit, Not Payment

Legalism turns obedience into currency—something offered to earn acceptance or maintain standing. The gospel reverses this order. In Christ, acceptance comes first; obedience follows as fruit.

"If you love me, you will keep my commandments."

—John 14:15

Obedience does not secure love; it expresses love. It is the visible outcome of a renewed heart, not the condition for belonging.

Jesus uses organic language to describe this reality:

"Whoever abides in me and I in him, he it is that bears much fruit."
— John 15:5

Fruit grows naturally from life. It cannot be forced. Likewise, obedience grows from union with Christ, not pressure to perform.

Reflection:

How does viewing obedience as fruit rather than payment change your motivation to obey?

Love as the Fulfillment of God's Will

Scripture makes a remarkable claim: what the Law demanded externally, love fulfills internally.

"Love is the fulfilling of the law."
— Romans 13:10

This does not mean love replaces holiness; it means love accomplishes holiness. Where love governs the heart, the will of God is expressed without coercion.

Paul summarizes this truth clearly:

"The whole law is fulfilled in one word: 'You shall love your neighbor as yourself.'"

— Galatians 5:14

Love does what law cannot: it aligns desire with righteousness. It moves obedience from obligation to joy.

Reflection:

Why does love succeed where fear-driven obedience fails?

Holiness Guarded from Two Errors

Understanding holiness without legalism protects believers from two extremes:

- Legalism, which burdens holiness with fear and performance

- Lawlessness, which mistakes grace for permission

Scripture rejects both. Grace produces holiness because it restores relationship, renews desire, and empowers obedience.

""For God has not called us for impurity, but in holiness."

— 1 Thessalonians 4:7

Chapter Summary

- Grace transforms the heart, not just behavior

- Obedience flows as fruit, not payment

- Love fulfills the will of God

- Holiness thrives without legalism

- True obedience grows from union with Christ

Final Reflection:

If holiness flows from grace rather than fear, how would your daily walk change if you lived fully from love instead of pressure?

End of Chapter 19

CHAPTER 20

Living By The Spirit

Life after the Law is not guided by fear, pressure, or self-regulation—it is lived by the Spirit. The Spirit does not replace truth; He applies it. He does not silence conscience; He renews it. And He does not sanctify through shame, but through truth and life.

"If we live by the Spirit, let us also keep in step with the Spirit."

— Galatians 5:25

This chapter explains how conscience is renewed, how growth occurs without condemnation, and how sanctification unfolds in truth rather than fear.

Conscience Renewed

Conscience is not an independent moral authority; it is a witness that must be shaped by truth. Left alone, conscience can be weak, distorted, or silenced. Renewed by the Spirit, conscience becomes aligned with God's revealed will.

"How much more will the blood of Christ… purify our conscience from dead works to serve the living God."

— Hebrews 9:14

The Spirit renews conscience by:

- Cleansing it from guilt already answered by Christ

- Reorienting it toward truth rather than fear

- Training it through Scripture and life in Christ

Paul speaks of a conscience informed by truth, not accusation:

""So I always take pains to have a clear conscience toward both God and man."

—Acts 24:16

A renewed conscience no longer condemns what Christ has forgiven, nor excuses what truth exposes.

Reflection:

How can conscience be both helpful and harmful if it is not continually shaped by God's truth?

Growth Without Shame

Shame is not a tool of sanctification. It may restrain behavior temporarily, but it cannot produce lasting transformation. Scripture consistently presents growth as the result of grace and truth, not humiliation.

"There is therefore now no condemnation for those who are in Christ Jesus."
— **Romans 8:1**

The Spirit convicts, but He does not condemn. Conviction draws the believer toward restoration; shame pushes the believer into hiding. Growth flourishes where safety and truth meet.

"But speaking the truth in love, we are to grow up in every way into him."
— **Ephesians 4:15**

When shame is removed, repentance becomes honest, and obedience becomes willing rather than defensive.

Reflection:

Why does growth stall when shame dominates instead of truth and grace?

Sanctification in Truth

Sanctification is not self-made holiness; it is life shaped by truth under the Spirit's guidance. Truth reveals reality as God sees it, and the Spirit applies that truth inwardly.

"Sanctify them in the truth; your word is truth."
— John 17:17

The Spirit uses truth to:

- Expose remaining misalignment
- Renew the mind
- Form Christlike character

Paul describes this ongoing renewal:

"Be transformed by the renewal of your mind."
— Romans 12:2

Sanctification is not instantaneous perfection; it is progressive conformity to Christ, grounded in life, not fear.

Reflection:

How does sanctification change when it is understood as life in truth rather than pressure to perform?

Why Living by the Spirit Completes Life After the Law

The Law could command holiness but could not produce it. The Spirit accomplishes what the Law could only describe.

"Walk by the Spirit, and you will not gratify the desires of the flesh."
— Galatians 5:16

Life after the Law is not ungoverned—it is Spirit-governed. This governance brings freedom, clarity, and growth rooted in truth.

Chapter Summary

- The Spirit renews conscience through truth

- Growth occurs without shame or condemnation

- Sanctification is life shaped by truth

- The Spirit applies what Christ has accomplished

- Living by the Spirit fulfills life after the Law

Final Reflection:

If the Spirit is shaping your conscience, growth, and sanctification, what would it look like to trust His work rather than relying on fear or self-effort?

End of Chapter 20

CHAPTER 21

A Life Reconciled To God

Salvation's final picture is not merely forgiven sinners, but reconciled people—standing in peace with God, living from mercy, and restored to life in Christ. Reconciliation brings together what sin divided and what the Law exposed: justice honored, mercy received, and life restored.

"Since we have been justified by faith, we have peace with God through our Lord Jesus Christ."
— Romans 5:1

This chapter gathers the whole message of salvation and shows what life looks like when reconciliation is not only believed, but lived.

Justice Honored

Reconciliation does not come by ignoring justice. It comes because justice has been fully satisfied. God does not reconcile by lowering His standard; He reconciles by meeting it in Christ.

"He made him to be sin who knew no sin, so that in him we might become the righteousness of God."

— 2 Corinthians 5:21

At the cross, God remains just while justifying sinners. The Law's demand is not dismissed; it is fulfilled. This is why reconciliation is secure—nothing unresolved remains between God and those in Christ.

"It was to show his righteousness… so that he might be just and the justifier."

— Romans 3:26

Reflection:

Why does reconciliation depend on justice being honored rather than overlooked?

Mercy Received

Because justice is satisfied, mercy can be freely given. Mercy is not indulgence; it is costly compassion grounded in truth.

"But God, being rich in mercy, because of the great love with which he loved us…"

— Ephesians 2:4

Mercy restores what guilt had broken. It invites the reconciled person to live not under suspicion, but under grace. Scripture describes this new standing boldly:

"Let us then with confidence draw near to the throne of grace."

— Hebrews 4:16

Mercy received becomes mercy lived. Those reconciled to God are freed from defensiveness and fear, able to extend grace to others.

Reflection:

How does confidence before God change the way you relate to Him—and to others?

Life Restored in Christ

Reconciliation is not merely a change in status; it is the restoration of life. What sin severed, Christ reunites. What death ruled, life now reigns.

"If while we were enemies we were reconciled to God by the death of his Son, much more… shall we be saved by his life."

— Romans 5:10

Life in Christ is relational, ongoing, and transforming. It is lived not in fear of judgment, but in communion with God.

"I am the vine; you are the branches… apart from me you can do nothing."

— John 15:5

This restored life expresses itself in peace, obedience born of love, and hope that reaches beyond death.

Reflection:

Where do you need to live more fully from restored life rather than from past brokenness?

Reconciliation as the Shape of Daily Life

A reconciled life is marked by:

- Peace with God, not fear of Him

- Confidence, not condemnation

- Love, not performance

Paul summarizes this calling:

"We implore you on behalf of Christ, be reconciled to God."

— 2 Corinthians 5:20

Those reconciled become ambassadors—living testimonies that justice and mercy meet in Christ.

Chapter Summary

- Reconciliation honors justice and receives mercy

- Peace with God replaces fear of judgment

- Life is restored through union with Christ

- Mercy received becomes mercy lived

- Reconciliation shapes everyday Christian life

Final Reflection:

If you are truly reconciled to God—justice satisfied, mercy received, life restored—what would it look like to live today from peace instead of striving?

End of Chapter 21

CONCLUSION

The Law Revealed The Truth—Salvation Accomplished

The Cure

From the beginning of Scripture to its final pages, one unified story unfolds. Humanity stands accountable before a holy God. Sin distorts, separates, and brings death. The Law enters history to make that condition unmistakably clear. And Christ arrives not to deny that truth—but to fulfill it and restore life.

The Law revealed the truth.

Salvation accomplished the cure.

Scripture Answered the Human Problem

The human problem is deeper than ignorance of rules. It is not merely behavioral failure; it is misalignment with God Himself. Long before Sinai, sin existed. Death reigned before commandments were written. Conscience bore witness, even when revelation was limited.

"Sin indeed was in the world before the law was given."

— Romans 5:13

The Law later clarified what was already true:

"Through the law comes knowledge of sin."
— **Romans 3:20**

It defined transgression. It silenced self-justification. It exposed guilt. It showed that justice must be satisfied. But Scripture is equally clear: the Law cannot give life.

"If a law had been given that could give life, then righteousness would indeed be by the law."
— **Galatians 3:21**

The Law diagnoses. It does not heal.

Christ Fulfilled What the Law Required

Jesus did not abolish the Law as false or unnecessary. He fulfilled it—bringing it to its intended goal.

"Do not think that I have come to abolish the Law or the Prophets… but to fulfill them."
— **Matthew 5:17**

He satisfied its justice.

He bore its curse.

He answered its charges.

He healed the deeper corruption of sin.

And once fulfilled, the Law's role as the path to righteousness ended—not because righteousness ended, but because its goal arrived.

"For Christ is the end of the law for righteousness to everyone who believes." — **Romans 10:4**

Faith now rests not in a system, not in performance, not in fear—but in a Person.

An Invitation to Life in Christ

This book has argued carefully and scripturally:

- Sin existed before written Law
- The Law reveals truth but cannot give life
- Transgression creates chargeable guilt
- Justice must be satisfied
- Christ fulfills what the Law required
- Salvation restores life and removes condemnation

The invitation is not toward lawlessness. It is toward life in Christ.

"There is therefore now no condemnation for those who are in Christ Jesus."

— Romans 8:1

"If anyone is in Christ, he is a new creation."

— 2 Corinthians 5:17

This is not a call to abandon holiness—but to find it where Scripture locates it: in union with Christ, empowered by the Spirit, grounded in grace.

The Law revealed the truth about us.

Christ reveals the mercy of God.

Salvation restores what sin destroyed.

Final Word

If you have trusted the Law for righteousness, look to Christ.

If you have lived under fear, rest in His finished work.

If you have wondered whether life can truly be restored, believe the gospel.

"Believe in the Lord Jesus, and you will be saved."

— Acts 16:31

The Law reveals the truth.

Christ fulfills the Law.

Salvation restores life.

And life is found in Him alone.

APPENDIX A

Biblical Definitions

This appendix provides clear, scriptural definitions of key terms used throughout this book. These definitions are not philosophical abstractions or theological inventions; they arise from Scripture interpreting Scripture. Precision here protects the gospel from confusion, legalism, and false assurance.

1. Sin

Biblical Definition:

Sin is relational and ontological misalignment with God—anything that does not conform to God's nature, will, truth, character, and life. Sin exists prior to written law and results in separation from God and the reign of death.

Sin is not first a legal violation; it is a condition of being out of alignment with God, the source of life.

"All have sinned and fall short of the glory of God."

— **Romans 3:23**

"Sin indeed was in the world before the law was given."

— **Romans 5:13**

Key Clarifications:

- Sin can exist without transgression

- Sin corrupts desire, mind, and relationship

- Sin results in death as consequence, not merely penalty

Summary:

Sin explains why humanity is broken.

2. Transgression

Biblical Definition:

Transgression is the violation of a known, revealed command of God. It is sin crossing a defined boundary, creating legal guilt and chargeable offense.

Transgression requires law.

"Where there is no law there is no transgression."
— Romans 4:15

"The law was added because of transgressions."
— Galatians 3:19

Key Clarifications:

- All transgression is sin

- Not all sin is transgression

- Transgression increases accountability where revelation increases

Summary:

Transgression explains why justice must be satisfied.

3. Law (Spiritual and Mosaic)

a. Spiritual Law (Uncodified)

Biblical Definition:

Spiritual law refers to the moral and relational order rooted in God's nature—His holiness, truth, righteousness, and life. It exists prior to written commandments and governs reality itself.

"Death reigned from Adam to Moses."

— Romans 5:14

This law explains why:

- Sin has consequences before Sinai

- Humanity experiences accountability apart from Torah

- Conscience bears witness (though imperfectly)

Clarification:

Spiritual law defines sin, but does not codify transgression.

b. Mosaic Law (Codified)

Biblical Definition:

The Mosaic Law is God's written, covenantal law given to Israel, defining commands, prohibitions, and penalties. It transforms sin into chargeable transgression and functions as witness, tutor, and judge.

"Through the law comes knowledge of sin."
— **Romans 3:20**

"The law was our guardian to bring us to Christ."
— **Galatians 3:24**

Limitations of the Law:

- It cannot give life

- It cannot heal the heart

- It cannot justify sinners

Summary:

The Law reveals truth—but Christ fulfills and completes it.

4. Justice

Biblical Definition:

Justice is God's unwavering commitment to uphold truth, righteousness, and moral order. Justice requires that wrongdoing be addressed—not ignored—and that guilt be answered.

"He will by no means clear the guilty."

— Exodus 34:7

Justice is not opposed to mercy. In Scripture, justice is the necessary foundation that makes mercy meaningful.

"So that he might be just and the justifier of the one who has faith in Jesus."

— Romans 3:26

Summary:

Justice explains why the cross was necessary.

5. Salvation

Biblical Definition:

Salvation is God's complete work in Christ by which justice is satisfied, sin is healed, relationship is restored, and life is given. Salvation is not earned by law-keeping; it is received by faith in Christ.

"For what the law could not do… God did by sending his own Son."

— Romans 8:3

Salvation includes:

- Justification (guilt answered)
- Reconciliation (relationship restored)
- New creation (life restored)
- Sanctification (life lived by the Spirit)

"If anyone is in Christ, he is a new creation."
— 2 Corinthians 5:17

Summary:

Salvation explains what the Law could never accomplish.

Appendix A Summary Table

- Sin → misalignment with God (condition)
- Transgression → violation of known law (charge)
- Law → reveals truth and defines accountability
- Justice → requires wrongdoing to be answered
- Salvation → fulfills justice and restores life in Christ

Final Statement

The Law reveals the truth.

Christ fulfills the Law.

Salvation restores life.

APPENDIX B

Doctrinal Questions

This appendix addresses some of the most common and consequential doctrinal questions that arise when discussing the Law, salvation, assurance, and Christian life. Each answer is grounded in Scripture, shaped by sound theology, and consistent with the central claim of this book: the Law leads to Christ, but Christ alone is the way of life.

1. Is the Law Still Binding?

Short Answer:

The Law is no longer binding as a covenantal system, but it remains true, holy, and fulfilled in Christ.

Scripture teaches that the Law's role was temporary and purposeful—to reveal sin, define transgression, and lead people to Christ.

"So then, the law was our guardian to bring us to Christ, that we might be justified by faith. But now that faith has come, we are no longer under a tutor."

— Galatians 3:24–25

Believers are not "under the Law" as a means of righteousness or covenantal obligation.

"For you are not under law but under grace."
— **Romans 6:14**

However, the Law is not discarded. It is fulfilled—its righteousness embodied in Christ and expressed in those who walk by the Spirit.

"In order that the righteous requirement of the law might be fulfilled in us, who walk not according to the flesh but according to the Spirit."
— **Romans 8:4**

Conclusion:

The Law no longer governs salvation or standing before God. Christ does.

2. Why Does Conviction Remain Without Condemnation?

Short Answer:

Because conviction restores, while condemnation destroys.

Conviction is the Spirit's work of exposing misalignment so that relationship and growth may continue. Condemnation is a legal verdict of guilt with no path forward—and it has been removed in Christ.

"When he comes, he will convict the world concerning sin and righteousness and judgment."

— John 16:8

"There is therefore now no condemnation for those who are in Christ Jesus."

— Romans 8:1

Conviction leads to repentance and renewal. Condemnation produces fear, hiding, and despair. Scripture clearly distinguishes the two.

Conclusion:

Conviction remains because God continues to transform His children.

Condemnation is removed because justice has been satisfied in Christ.

3. Can Salvation Be Lost?

Short Answer:

Salvation is secure because it rests on Christ's finished work, not human consistency.

If salvation depended on human performance, it would never be secure. Scripture repeatedly anchors assurance in what God has done and continues to do in Christ.

"By a single offering he has perfected for all time those who are being sanctified."

— **Hebrews 10:14**

"Who shall bring any charge against God's elect? It is God who justifies."

— **Romans 8:33**

Warnings in Scripture function as means of perseverance, not evidence that salvation is fragile. They call believers to remain in Christ, not to live in fear of abandonment.

"He who began a good work in you will bring it to completion."

— **Philippians 1:6**

Conclusion:

Salvation is secure because Christ's work is complete and God's promise is faithful.

4. What Does "Fulfillment" Truly Mean?

Short Answer:

Fulfillment means completion, satisfaction, and arrival at the intended goal—not cancellation or disregard.

Jesus explicitly defined His mission in relation to the Law:

"Do not think that I have come to abolish the Law or the Prophets; I have not come to abolish them but to fulfill them."

— Matthew 5:17

Fulfillment means:

- The Law's righteousness is accomplished

- The Law's justice is satisfied

- The Law's purpose is completed

Paul summarizes this clearly:

"For Christ is the end of the law for righteousness to everyone who believes."

— Romans 10:4

The Law pointed forward. Christ arrived. Faith must now rest in Him, not in the Law as a system.

Conclusion:

Fulfillment does not weaken the Law—it honors it by completing it.

Appendix B Summary

- The Law is fulfilled in Christ and no longer governs salvation

- Conviction remains for growth; condemnation is removed by grace

- Salvation is secure because it rests on Christ's finished work

- Fulfillment means completion, not cancellation

Final Clarifying Statement

The Law leads to Christ.

Christ fulfills the Law.

Salvation rests in Him alone.

APPENDIX C

The Scriptural Framework

Sin → Law → Transgression → Christ → Life

This Scriptural framework summarizes the biblical logic of redemption presented throughout this book. Scripture does not treat sin, law, transgression, and salvation as competing ideas, but as a progressive revelation that leads decisively to Christ and culminates in life.

1. Sin — The Human Condition (Before and Beyond Law)

What Scripture Reveals:

Sin is humanity's relational and ontological misalignment with God. It exists prior to written law and results in separation from God and the reign of death.

"All have sinned and fall short of the glory of God."

— Romans 3:23

"Sin indeed was in the world before the law was given."

— Romans 5:13

Key Truth:

Sin explains why humanity is broken—even where no command has been violated.

2. Law — Revelation of Truth and Accountability

What Scripture Reveals:

The Law is God's revealed standard, given to make sin unmistakable, define righteousness, and clarify accountability. The Law does not create sin; it exposes it.

"Through the law comes knowledge of sin."
— Romans 3:20

"The law was added because of transgressions."
— Galatians 3:19

Key Truth:

The Law reveals truth, but cannot give life.

3. Transgression — Sin Made Chargeable

What Scripture Reveals:

Transgression occurs when sin crosses a known boundary. It is the legal violation of revealed command and creates judicial guilt.

"Where there is no law there is no transgression."

— Romans 4:15

Key Truth:

Transgression explains why justice must be satisfied.

4. Christ — Fulfillment, Not Cancellation

What Scripture Reveals:

Christ fulfills the Law by satisfying its justice, answering transgression, and healing sin. The Law's purpose reaches completion in Him.

"Do not think that I have come to abolish the Law... but to fulfill them."

— Matthew 5:17

"For Christ is the end of the law for righteousness to everyone who believes."

— Romans 10:4

Key Truth:

Faith must now move from Law-trust to Christ-trust.

5. Life — Salvation Accomplished

What Scripture Reveals:

In Christ, condemnation ends, relationship is restored, and life replaces death. Salvation is not achieved by law-keeping but received through union with Christ.

"There is therefore now no condemnation for those who are in Christ Jesus."

— Romans 8:1

"If anyone is in Christ, he is a new creation."

— 2 Corinthians 5:17

Key Truth:

Life is the goal—not law, not fear, not performance.

The Complete Flow (At a Glance)

- Sin → reveals humanity's broken condition

- Law → reveals truth and accountability

- Transgression → creates legal guilt

- Christ → fulfills the Law and satisfies justice

- Life → restored relationship, new creation, freedom

Final Summary Statement

- The Law reveals the truth about sin.

- Christ fulfills the Law.

- Salvation restores life.

This is the scriptural framework of redemption—from beginning to end.

SCRIPTURAL INDEX

The following index lists all primary Scripture references used throughout this book, organized in canonical order. This index allows readers, teachers, and students to trace the biblical foundation of each doctrinal argument and to verify that Scripture answers Scripture from beginning to end.

Old Testament

Genesis

Exodus

Leviticus

Purpose of This Index

This Scripture Index demonstrates that:

- Sin exists before the Law

- The Law reveals truth but cannot give life

- Transgression creates legal guilt

- Christ fulfills the Law and satisfies justice

- Salvation restores life and relationship

- Assurance rests on Christ, not performance

Every doctrinal conclusion in this book is anchored in the whole counsel of Scripture, not isolated verses or theological preference.

Final Index Summary

From Genesis to Revelation, Scripture tells one story:

- The Law reveals the truth.

- Christ fulfills the Law.

- Salvation restores life.

SUBJECT INDEX

This Subject Index organizes the major theological, biblical, and doctrinal themes addressed throughout Salvation and the Law. It is designed to help readers quickly locate discussions, trace arguments, and teach or study specific topics with clarity.

A

Accountability

– before written Law, xix—xxii

– moral accountability before God, xi, xix—xxii

– clarified by Law, xxii, 35 –52

Accusation

– accusation and false assurance, 89–102

– relationship to condemnation, 53–57

– answered through Christ, 109–125

Assurance of Salvation

– false assurance contrasted, 89–102

– security through Christ, 133–155

– relationship to condemnation, 133–143

G

God

– source of truth, justice, and goodness, 1–6

– foundation of morality, 1–6

– relationship to humanity, xix—xxviii, 157-181

Goodness

– rooted in God's nature, 1–6

– reflected in Law, 1–6

Grace

– relationship to holiness, 139–144

– transformation of life, 145–156

Guilt

– awareness of guilt, x—xi, xix-xxviii

– guilt defined by Law, 35—57

– guilt answered through Christ, 109--119

H

Heart

– Law written on the heart, 21–34

– relationship to conscience, 21–34

– exposed by Law, 18—52

L

Law

– before Sinai, 1–34

– purpose of Law, 35–40

– reveals sin, 41–46

– defines transgression, 47–57

– limits of Law, 59–70

– fulfilled in Christ, 103–131

Law Written on the Heart

– moral awareness before written Law, 21–34

– relationship to conscience, xix—xxviii

Life

– restored through Christ, 133—154

– internal life replacing external Law, 121–131

– reconciled life, 151–155

Love

– fulfillment of holiness, 139–143

– expression of reconciled life, 151–155

Truth

– rooted in God's nature, 1–6

– revealed by Law, 35–46 ·

– fulfilled in Christ, 103–131

U

Union with Christ

– life in Christ, 121–155

– foundation of transformation, 145–155

W

Written Law

– distinction from moral awareness, xix—xxviii

– clarifies truth, xxii—xxviii

– defines transgression, xii, xxii—xxvii

Final Index Statement

This index reflects a single biblical truth:

- The Law reveals the truth.

- Christ fulfills the Law.

- Salvation restores life.

ACKNOWLEDGEMENTS

All glory and gratitude belong first to God the Father, who reveals truth; to Jesus Christ, who fulfilled the Law and accomplished salvation; and to the Holy Spirit, who leads into truth and gives life. Without God's revelation, none of this would be understood. Without His mercy, none of us would stand.

I am deeply thankful for the Scriptures, the living and coherent Word of God, which does not contradict itself but unfolds one unified story—from sin to Law to Christ to life. Every page of this book is an attempt to let Scripture speak for itself, to allow its own progression and clarity to shape the theology presented here.

To the pastors, teachers, and faithful servants of Christ who have handled God's Word with reverence and integrity—thank you. Though this work stands on Scripture alone as its authority, it has been sharpened through conversations, teaching, and the example of those who love truth more than tradition and Christ more than systems.

To my church family and ministry community, your questions, struggles, hunger for understanding, and desire for freedom in Christ have deeply influenced this book. Many of the themes explored here were refined through pastoral conversations, prayer, and the shared pursuit of clarity in the gospel.

To my family, thank you for your patience, encouragement, and unwavering support. Your love has been a constant reminder that theology is not merely to be studied—but lived with humility, grace, and devotion to Christ.

Finally, to every reader, thank you for engaging these pages thoughtfully. My prayer is not simply that you would gain understanding, but that you would experience freedom—freedom from fear, freedom from condemnation, and freedom to walk in the life Christ gives.

"You will know the truth, and the truth will set you free."
— John 8:32

May this book serve one purpose above all:

- That Christ would be trusted.

- That justice would be understood.

- That mercy would be received.

And that salvation would be lived.

ABOUT THE AUTHOR

Dr. Ed Grefiel is a Christian teacher, pastor, and author committed to presenting the gospel with biblical faithfulness, theological clarity, and pastoral care. His work centers on helping people understand salvation not as religious performance, but as life restored through the finished work of Jesus Christ.

With a deep passion for Scripture, Dr. Grefiel approaches theology as a unified story in which Scripture interprets Scripture, Christ stands at the center, and truth is never separated from love. His teaching consistently emphasizes the distinction—and proper relationship—between sin and transgression, Law and grace, justice and mercy, and obedience and life in the Spirit.

Dr. Grefiel writes for all people, not only for the church—addressing universal questions of conscience, guilt, accountability, justice, and hope that every human heart encounters. His goal is to remove fear-based religion and replace it with assurance grounded in Christ, calling readers to move from trusting systems to trusting a Person.

He is the author of multiple works exploring salvation, assurance, sin, grace, and the life of faith, including books written for pastors, leaders, and everyday readers seeking clarity and freedom in Christ. Across all his writing, one conviction remains constant:

The Law reveals the truth.

Christ fulfills the Law.

Salvation restores life.

Dr. Grefiel continues to teach, write, and serve the Christian community with a desire to see people freed from condemnation, rooted in truth, and living fully in the life Christ gives.

CONTINUE THE JOURNEY

Steps of Faith: A Journey to Salvation For All is a developing twelve-book series centered on salvation through Jesus Christ.

Written progressively beginning in 2014 through years of Bible study, teaching, and gospel-centered discussions. These books continue to be taught and shared today.

Available and Upcoming Releases

- *Understanding Salvation as the Foundation of Everything*

- *Salvation and the Law: What the Law Can Do—and What Salvation Alone Can Accomplish (Current Volume)*

- *Turning to Christ: Faith, Repentance, and the Grace That Saves*

- *God's Mercy and Grace*

    - *Saved by Mercy, Held by Grace: Understanding the Salvation of Children Through Christ Alone*

    - *The Unstoppable Power of Mercy and Grace: Mercy, Grace, and Salvation in the Redemptive Work of Christ*

- *The Unshakable Assurance of Salvation: Held by the Finished Work of Christ*

Additional volumes in the *Steps of Faith* series are currently in development.

The Law was fulfilled.

The debt was answered.

Life has come through Christ.

Continue in Christ.

Walk in truth.

Hold firmly to Him alone.

www.ingramcontent.com/pod-product-compliance
Lightning Source LLC
Chambersburg PA
CBHW071503140726
47997CB00005B/1840